LUFTWAFFE AIRCRAFT

MICHAEL TURNER
'85

LUFTWAFFE AIRCRAFT

Paintings by Michael Turner

Commentary by Frank Mason

TEMPLE PRESS

NEWNES BOOKS

To Graham, Alison and Suzanne

Published by Temple Press
an imprint of Newnes Books
a division of The Hamlyn Publishing Group Limited
Bridge House, 69 London Road, Twickenham, Middlesex, TW1 3SB
and distributed for them by
Hamlyn Distribution Services
Rushden, Northants, England

ISBN 0 600 35154 8

Printed in Italy

Contents

Foreword

I was five years old when the Second World War broke out in 1939, and my growing interest in aeroplanes was accelerated by patriotic fervour, directed particularly to the exploits of the Royal Air Force.

The Luftwaffe, thankfully the only arm of the Axis powers to come anywhere near making personal contact, when it threatened our wellbeing by dropping bombs around our house in the London suburbs, held by contrast a sinister fascination. The monotonous throbbing of unsynchronized engines droning overhead during the blitz, the excitement tinged with fear when we saw an He 111 caught in the searchlight beams above our house, the collecting of bomb fragments from the gutters on the way to school, and the viewing of shot-down German aircraft on display all coloured my youthful imagination. Only in later years, of course, did I become more fully aware of the horrors of the two World Wars, and the realities and implications are not to be treated lightly or ever forgotten.

The work in this book, however, is intended to be a representative record of a selection of the flying machines used and developed by the German Air Forces in many guises and varying operating conditions, following their fluctuating fortunes through a momentous period of history. It will, I hope, provide a logical follow-up to my earlier volume featuring aircraft of the Royal Air Force.

I am indebted to Frank Mason for complementing my paintings and drawings so well with an informative and entertaining narrative.

M.T.

Introduction

It has been said that the Western nations had only themselves to blame for the rise to power of Adolf Hitler. For the moment the ink dried on the signatures to the Treaty of Versailles the seeds of resentment were sown throughout a nation already seething with frustration and strife, a nation whose very life-giving industries were to be seized as retribution for a war that had taken the lives of a whole generation. And history down the ages had demonstrated that Treaties without teeth only breed greater trouble.

Germany has never lacked brilliant men and brave soldiers, the ingredients to generate wealth and to defend it. Her air force in the First World War possessed men and machines second to none, great men who created a tradition of bravery and skill that has survived to this day: pride in their unit, pride in their country–these are not human attributes that disappear under the weight of a humiliating Treaty. So it must be said that when a leader emerged, as Hitler did in 1933, who promised order where chaos reigned, pride in the nation where lack of direction had characterised successive governments, it was the most natural consequence for the German people to rally to the national flag. Discipline is of first nature to the Germanic races–would that others were as well endowed–and the men who climbed so enthusiastically into the cockpit of their re-born air force had no reason to contemplate any sinister motivation. There was a gulf of difference between the outlook of the professional airman and the activities and political philosophies of the Party.

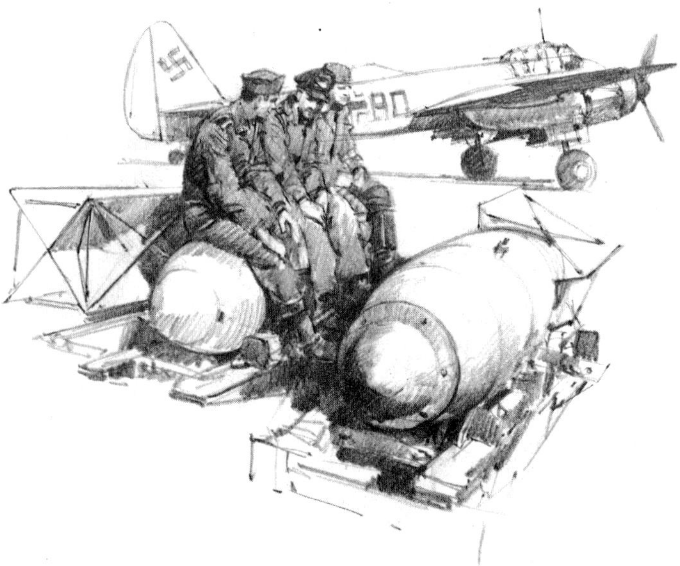

From the moment of the German Air Force's re-birth the Luftwaffe was professional in the extreme–perhaps somewhat removed from the 'best flying club in the world' that weaned brave but delightfully languid British airmen–for every German knew that since the collapse of the Geneva Disarmament Conference time was running out in Europe. Certainly Hitler's territorial ambitions, not least his hatred of the communist bear in the east, had set the Continent on the slippery slope to disaster.

And when the order was sounded, accompanied by all the trumpeting of modern propaganda, the Luftwaffe was ready; Europe was not. Calculating for a 'lightning war' of two years' duration, Göring had certainly given his Führer a magnificent air force–tailored exactly to the demands of Blitzkrieg. Whether a prolonged war against, and invasion of, Britain ever seriously entered Hitler's plans will forever remain unknown for certain; what was common knowledge was the Nazi leader's determination on a swift and crushing campaign against the hated Soviet Union. When *Barbarossa* stalled before the gates of Moscow not even the mighty Luftwaffe could get the machine moving forward once more. From that moment Germany, with war on three fronts, was probably doomed to ultimate defeat. Yet for three more years, facing the fast-growing strength of the British Commonwealth, the United States of America and the Soviet Union, the Luftwaffe fought on, sustained by fighting airmen of tremendous courage and with aircraft that were still a match for any adversary.

Although this book is primarily one that portrays the machinery of warfare, it is not intended to be a technical catalogue, or for that matter a comprehensive historical work of reference. Warfare, for all its bestiality, frequently thrusts Mankind's other, finer qualities to the fore: unselfishness, courage and comradeship. War is a series of episodes–often of terrible consequence, often of suffering, occasionally of wonderful endeavour. Seldom can such episodes be recaptured by the camera, for all facets of the common photograph are reduced to mechanical equality. The licence of the paintbrush, being a projection of the human senses, permits a sense of speed or tranquility, a focus on hazard and drama, of sudden light or pervading gloom; it is an enabling of interpretation. Our book thus seeks in picture and word to comment on the progress along the path of aviation by one of history's great fighting forces.

79

AIRCRAFT OF THE GERMAN AIR FORCE

Friedrichshafen seaplanes

The First Fighter – Fokker E I-III (Eindecker)

The eruption of the First World War in August 1914 found Germany with a collection of aeroplanes no less varied nor less suited for air warfare than Britain and France. But while Britain's War Office had forbidden the use of monoplanes (following some accidents just before the War), no such constraints were evident elsewhere. Indeed the *Feldfliegerabteilungen* (Fl Abt), which were integral components of the German Army, possessed more than fifty monoplanes at the outbreak of war–LVG, Jeannin, Kondor and Krieger aeroplanes, generically referred to as *Tauben* (Pigeons)–for general observation duties over the ground battles.

Few regarded seriously the likelihood of combat between aeroplanes, and for several months these observation duties were performed by both sides with seldom more than a chance encounter between opposing aircraft, the relatively difficult business of hitting the opponent with a rifle or pistol causing little interference with the job in hand. Nevertheless all three air forces in the West were experimenting with machine guns, fixed to fire forward. The British chose to mount their guns to fire outside the propeller arc, which made aiming difficult; the French produced a system by which the machine gun fired without interruption through the revolving propeller, the blades of which were fitted with steel deflector plates to prevent damage from occasional contact with the bullets.

In Germany however the idea of a 'synchronised' machine gun had been pursued before the War–that is a gun whose firing was mechanically timed to fire each round without striking the propeller blades. When the Dutchman Anthony Fokker persuaded the German authorities that a similar design fitted in his own A III monoplane provided self-defence for observation aircraft, he was authorised to build an example for official evaluation. After Fokker had himself demonstrated the prototype E I (for *Eindecker*, literally 'one wing'), it was put into limited production in the spring of 1915, single examples being distributed among the observation units on the Western Front. Among these was Fl Abt 62, commanded by the much

Max Immelmann was the first German airman to be idolised by the public for his prowess as a 'fighter pilot' although his mentor, Oswald Boelcke, was the true genius

respected Hauptmann Kastner and numbering among its pilots one Leutnant Oswald Boelcke.

Boelcke, already holder of the Iron Cross and an experienced observation pilot, quickly acquired considerable skill with the new single-seater, a proficiency that enabled him to adopt more aggressive tactics, seeking out Allied aircraft and attacking them. In May another young man who was to gain immortal fame, Max Immelmann, joined Fl Abt 62 and soon a strong partnership developed, Boelcke assuming the rôles of tactician and mentor, and Immelmann the brilliant student. The Kastner-Boelcke-Immelmann team was soon able to demonstrate that, with careful schooling in elementary tactics, it was possible to *attack* enemy aeroplanes and shoot them down.

First victory by a Fokker E I went to Immelmann on August 1, 1915 when he shot down a British two-seater flown by Lt William Reid near Douai – a rather hollow triumph as the RFC machine was on a bombing flight without an observer, and therefore defenceless. Nevertheless, although the E I suffered its share of mechanical troubles, air victories began to mount and these encouraged the immediate introduction of improved versions, the E II and III with more powerful Oberursel rotary engines and improved wing design. The monoplane was essentially a very simple aeroplane, the mid-mounted wing deriving its strength from external bracing wires between the spars and pylons located above and below the fuselage ahead of the cockpit. Of all the versions to reach the Western Front the E III was the most popular among the pilots, although the little monoplane was undoubtedly tricky to fly. Yet men like Boelcke, who is generally regarded as the father of air combat tactics and who shot or 'forced' down 40 Allied aircraft by the date of his death on October 28, 1916, mastered the art of stalking their prey and despatching their victims with a well-aimed burst of fire from their single gun. Immelmann, perhaps a most instinctive pilot, gave his name to the manoeuvre which he so often employed in combat: pulling up after his first burst of fire and winging over to dive down in the opposite direction for a second attack; his score stood at 15 when his aircraft, an E III, broke up during combat on June 18, 1916. Both these early 'aces' won the coveted *Pour le Mérite* and their names have been perpetuated in the honour titles of *Geschwader* in today's Luftwaffe.

The total number of Fokker monoplanes delivered to the Western Front was no more than 180. Yet for more than nine months this Fokker's supremacy was absolute: woe betide any Allied airman who failed to scan the skies for, once attacked, only a jammed Parabellum gun would bring salvation.

V-Strutters – Albatross D III

It has frequently been averred that the first appearance of the aeroplane over the ground battle manifested the onset of true mechanical warfare. It frightened the horses. It certainly sparked a scientific pattern of weapon and counter-weapon that has continued to this day. The dominance of the skies by the German monoplanes in 1915 forced the Allies to seek an antidote to the Fokker 'scourge', and in due course the initiative was wrested by fighting scouts, as they became known, such as the D.H.2 and Nieuports. By the summer of 1916 the Allies were once more in the ascendancy over the holocaust of Verdun and the Somme.

The little *Eindecker* had been basically sound, but it was realized that it was too light and its construction too primitive for it to withstand the rigours of the dogfight. Instead the newly created *Deutsche Luftstreitkraft* (German Air Force) turned to the more established biplane formula for its new fighting scouts, and it was with such aeroplanes as the Albatros D I and D II that the new *Jagdstaffeln* (*Jastas*, or fighter squadrons) began to regain superiority over the Western Front. With their smoothly contoured, semi-monocoque ply-clad fuselage, single-bay wings and 160-hp Mercedes water-cooled engines, the D II was almost 30 miles per hour faster than the *Eindecker* and possessed an armament increased to two synchronised machine guns. By the end of the year the *Jastas* had regained superiority over their Allied opponents, albeit at some cost for while leading *Jasta 2* in one of these biplanes on October 28, 1916 Boelcke died when he and his wingman, Erwin Böhme, collided.

Scourge of the Allied air forces in the spring of 1917, the beautifully steamlined Albatros D III was the mount of numerous high scoring German fighter pilots, led by von Richthofen himself

Encouraged by the early tests of the Albatros D II the *Luftstreitkraft* quickly ordered a further improved version, the D III. By raising the compression ratio of the engine, power was increased to 175 hp. The redesign of the wings was drastic, the lower wing being much reduced in chord and the tips being given a swept, elliptical planform. The engine radiator, formerly on the sides of the fuselage, was moved to the top wing. Although slightly slower than the D II, the later aircraft was a much better fighting machine, its manoeuvrability having been transformed and the pilot afforded a much improved field of view.

Production of the D III got under way quickly early in 1917, at first joining but soon replacing the D I and D II. From the outset the new scout earned the nickname 'vee-strutter' among RFC pilots on account of the V-interplane struts, a sobriquet that was quickly to reflect a passionate respect for the German aircraft. Now flown in formations of up to a dozen D IIIs, the new scouts proved deadly, particularly in the hands of the rising generation of young, newly trained pilots. The greatest of these was unquestionably Manfred, Freiherr von Richthofen, eldest son of an aristocratic Prussian family, who had been groomed for combat by Boelcke himself in *Jasta 2* during the summer of 1916, and who had shot down the famous British pilot, Major Lanoe Hawker VC on November 23. By early 1917 he had been given command of *Jasta 11* with Albatros D IIIs, and in the month that became inscribed in British annals as 'Bloody April' the Albatros-equipped *Jastas* took enormous toll of RFC BE 2Cs and RE 8s; for example on the 13th of that month six RE 8s of No 59 Squadron RFC, engaged in photographing the Drocourt-Quéant railway, were attacked by six D IIIs of *Jasta 11*, led by von Richthofen, and all were shot down within minutes. In those thirty terrible days the RFC lost 316 pilots and observers, the great majority to the guns of the Albatros.

There is no doubt but that his aristocratic background, with its hunting and riding proclivities as well as his former cavalry service, imbued von Richthofen with all the instincts of a brilliant fighting scout pilot, able to lead men of similar character into battle. At the time of the great air fights of April 1917 over the Western Front, *Jasta 11* (as well as some other units) took to painting its aircraft in distinctive colour schemes to aid instant recognition of comrades during combat (von Richthofen's D III was predominantly red, Leutnant Karl-Emil Schaefer flew an aircraft with a black tail, and Manfred's younger brother, Lothar von Richthofen, flew a D III with prominent yellow markings). This period–the spring of 1917–was the heyday of German air combat fortunes in the First World War as scores of Albatros pilots reached and passed the magic figure of five victories to become officially recognised as 'aces'. By April no fewer than 37 *Jastas* had been created, the majority flying the D III. In June however, as signs appeared that new British and French scouts (such as the Sopwith Triplane and Spad S VII) were once more contesting German air superiority, the famous so-called 'Richthofen Circus' came into being near Cambrai, comprising four *Jastas*, enabling as many as 50 scouts to overwhelm the generally smaller formations of British and French aircraft in a single combat. While this and other *Geschwader* (Wings) continued to take heavy toll of Allied aircraft for some weeks, the superiority of the D III finally ended with the RFC's introduction of the SE 5A and Sopwith Camel towards the end of the summer.

A Brandenburg W12 taxies alongside a U-boat in the North Sea. 146 of these useful seaplanes served at Belgian and North German ports during 1917 and 1918

Seaplanes over the German Bay – the Hansa Brandenburgs

The firm of Hansa und Brandenburg was best known for its prolific output of seaplanes for the Central Powers, largely from the drawing board of that doyen of German aviation, Ernst Heinkel. Formerly a German company, it was purchased by the Trieste millionaire Camilo Castiglione who secured the services of Heinkel as chief designer from the Albatros concern in 1915. Thereafter all manner of floatplanes and flying boats were produced at the works on the Havel river west of Berlin, ranging from single- and two-seat scouts, torpedo bombers and even a tiny single-seat flying boat designed to be carried aboard U-boats. These and the company's other products served with the air forces and navies of Germany, Austro-Hungary and Italy.

Among the most widely used of Heinkel's Branden-

burg aircraft was the family of fighting seaplanes which had commenced with the KDW (*Kampf Doppeldecker Wasserflugzeug*)—itself a float-equipped version of the famous 'star-strutter' single-seat scout produced for the Austrian Army in 1916. Although the KDW continued in service until the end of the War, Heinkel was asked to produce a larger two-seater with rear defence, capable not only of use as a fighter but as a general purpose coastal seaplane for service over the North Sea and Baltic. First flown at Warnemunde on the Baltic in January 1917—the Havel being frozen over—the W 12 seaplane later entered service with either Benz or Mercedes water-cooled engines.

Arrival of W 12s at the Zeebrugge seaplane station was hailed with enthusiasm by *Marinekorps Gruppe 1* whose pilots had been unable to counter the activities of the large, well-armed British flying boats. Commanding the Zeebrugge unit was Oberleutnant Friedrich ('Fiede') Christiansen, a 37-year-old naval officer who had gained his pilot's certificate shortly before the War. Under Christiansen's leadership the Brandenburg W 12 crews now set about a series of operations that was perhaps without equal during the War.

Occasionally venturing into British coastal waters for reconnaissance duties as well as escort for Friedrichshafen seaplanes, the W 12s were also used for short-range contact duties with U-boats at sea. More often however they were employed to intercept British and French bombing aircraft attempting to attack Zeebrugge itself as well as interfering with Allied flying boat patrols over the North Sea. On December 11, 1917 Christiansen himself shot down the British non-rigid coastal airship C27 in flames off the East Anglian coast; the following day he was awarded the *Pour le Mérite*, the only such award made to a naval aeroplane pilot. Among Christiansen's other claims was the British submarine C25, although unbeknown to the seaplane pilot she managed to limp home. Another British coastal airship, the C26, was also shot down by one of Christiansen's pilots.

To protect his seaplanes from bombing attacks on Zeebrugge Christiansen kept them in the railway sheds ashore on which a thick layer of reinforced concrete had been laid. When required for flying operations the aircraft were shunted out on flatbed railway trucks along the famous Mole and lifted into the water by quayside cranes. Thus the seaplane operations were hardly affected by the famous night raid by ships and men of the Royal Navy of April 22-23, 1918. Indeed, for just such an eventuality Christiansen had kept a locomotive with constant steam up so that when the British ships approached he simply had the aircraft withdrawn inland. Two days later the doughty commander exacted swift revenge for the raid by shooting down a Felixstowe F 2a flying boat.

June 1918 brought several big air battles with the F 2a flying boats. On the 4th five such aircraft had set out for Borkum from Felixstowe and Yarmouth, losing one which was forced to alight with a broken fuel pipe. The remaining four were soon attacked by 15 Brandenburg seaplanes. Two of the latter were brought down in the ensuing fight; one of the flying boats was forced to alight, its crew being interned by the Dutch. The seaplanes then shot up the original F 2a whose crew was struggling to repair the broken fuel pipe and who put up a spirited defence from the sea, shooting down another Brandenburg. The boat was eventually set on fire as it taxied towards Terschelling, its crew being interned.

On another occasion a Felixstowe was shot down by five Brandenburgs; the British boat captain, Lt-Col Robertson, climbed on his upturned hull as one of the seaplanes alighted and taxied up. The German pilot offered Robertson the choice of a lift to Zeebrugge and captivity or awaiting a chance rescue by an Allied vessel, to which the colonel replied that he preferred the latter. The seaplane pilot then took a photograph of the British pilot on his wreck, waved farewell and returned to his own base.

New Brandenburg seaplanes arrived in service in 1918, including the W 19 (an enlarged improvement of the W 12) and the W 29 monoplane. On August 11 a patrol of 14 W 29s from Borkum encountered a flotilla of six coastal motor boats, destroying three with machine gun fire and forcing the other three to beach in Holland where their crews were interned.

By the end of the War Christiansen's score stood at 21 aeroplanes shot down. During the Second World War he headed the military government in occupied Holland, and was afterwards charged by the Allies for atrocities committed by the SS; imprisoned, he later received a pardon to live out his old age in retirement in Western Germany.

Fokker Dr I Triplane

Goaded by frequent reports from the Western Front of the remarkable manoeuvrability of the new Sopwith Triplane during the early spring of 1917, the *Flugzeugmeisterei* invited almost every member of the German aircraft industry to tender similar designs, such essays eventually emerging from AEG, Brandenburg, DFW, Euler, LFG, Roland, Pfalz, Schütte-Lanz and Siemens-Schuckert. However Anthony Fokker personally visited *Jasta 11*, and was regaled with accounts of the fight between a lone Sopwith Triplane (flown by Lt R. A. Little of No 8 Squadron RNAS) and the *Jasta's* 11 Albatros D IIIs on April 7 when the British scout outmanoeuvred them all. Fokker instructed his chief designer, Reinhold Platz, to design a similar scout around the French 110-hp Le Rhone rotary engine, knowing that a large stock of these (ordered from the Swedish Thulin company) were being held at Adlershof, and that Oberursel was engaged in tooling up to produce a copy. When first flown the Fokker Dr I (Dr for *Dreidecker*, three wings) dispensed with interplane struts, but Fokker himself demanded their introduction, as well as a number of other alterations.

The first two Dr Is (actually prototype aircraft) were officially accepted on August 16 and five days later were delivered to von Richthofen's 'circus', *Jagdgeschwader Nr 1* (comprising *Jastas 4, 6, 10* and *11*) at Courtrai. Although flown by several different pilots, these first two Triplanes became virtually the personal mounts of von Richthofen himself and Leutnant Werner Voss, leader of *Jasta 10*. The Dr I scored its first success when Voss shot down a British aircraft on August 30, the first of 21 victories gained by this brilliant pilot in a period of just over three weeks; on September 23, flying his original Dr I, Voss met his death in an epic fight with the SE 5As of 'B' Flight, No 56 Squadron RFC. With a total of 48 victories to his credit and holder of the *Pour le Mérite*, Voss ranked fourth highest scorer among Germany's great scout pilots. In the other aircraft von Richthofen had claimed his 60th victim on September 1, but on the 15th it was shot down by Camels of No 10 Squadron RNAS while being flown by Oberleutnant Kurt Wolff of *Jasta 11*, who was killed (yet another holder of the 'Blue Max' with 33 victories).

Deliveries of production machines got under way in October, but before the end of that month two fatal accidents (one claiming the life of *Jasta 15* leader Heinrich Gontermann) resulted in the Triplanes being grounded. Inspection of other aircraft revealed poor workmanship and skimped production inspection–particularly of the wings–resulting in replacement by improved components. The accidents had nevertheless failed to dampen the enthusiasm of

Following pages: *the epic fight on September 23, 1917 between Werner Voss and McCudden's SE 5A; minutes later the German ace was to be shot down by another RFC pilot, Rhys-David*

V
MICHAEL TURNER

Fok.FI 103/17

the *Jasta* pilots for the little scout and long before the end of the year the Triplane was back in action once more.

Like the Sopwith Triplane, the Fokker possessed superb manoeuvrability, proving ideal in the combat conditions that had developed during 1917. It was at least a match for the average Allied pilot in the SE 5A, Spad S VII and Bristol Fighter–unless he chose to run away, when his aircraft could outpace the Dr I. Indeed it was in the close-in dogfight that the Dr I excelled, being armed with two synchronised machine guns in contrast to the single gun in most Sopwith Triplanes. Most of the leading German *Aberkanonen* were able to use it to add substantially to their victory tallies, among them the Richthofen brothers, Adolf Ritter von Tutschek and Ernst Udet.

All the early Dr Is were powered by Thulin-built Le Rhone rotaries and, in an effort to protect its licence agreement with France, the Swedish company fitted plates to its engines declaring that they had been salvaged from crashed aircraft, and this resulted in the engines being referred to as *Beute* units (booty). Although Oberursel-built engines (a company in which Fokker was the major shareholder) became available late in 1917 the *Jastas* expressed a strong preference for the Swedish product and the pilots went to considerable trouble to obtain *Beute* engines for themselves!

Various other engines were tried but the Triplane's top speed proved inadequate to match the performance of Allied scouts above about 13,000 ft despite its outstanding manoeuvrability. In May 1918 production was halted, the month after its greatest exponent had met his death in the cockpit of one. On April 21 Manfred von Richthofen was on patrol by himself in his famous red Triplane near the Bray-Corbie road when he was seen to attack two Sopwith Camels at very low altitude; some machine gunners on the ground opened fire, causing the German pilot to break off the attack and almost immediately strike the ground. When Allied troops reached the wreckage of the Triplane they found the pilot dead in his cockpit, shot through the head. It has been said that another Camel, flown by the Canadian Captain Roy Brown, attacked von Richthofen but this was not witnessed from the ground; nevertheless, although Brown was credited with shooting down the Fokker, controversy has raged to this day as to the true manner in which the great German pilot met his death. Certainly neither of the other two Camels were responsible–for it was established beyond question that their guns had jammed *before* being attacked by von Richthofen.

The Giants – Gotha G IV and Zeppelin-Staaken R VI

Less frequently called to mind than the activities of the nimble fighting scouts over the Western Front is the more sinister part played in the First World War by the bombers, or 'battleplanes' as they were more usually called by the Central Powers. Yet it was the Russians who initiated this rôle of the aeroplane–simply because, in their big Sikorsky aircraft, they already possessed a bomber capable of reaching beyond the immediate battlefield to deliver high explosive against the enemy's lines of communication. The Germans were not slow to emulate this unpleasant manifestation of '*la guerre totale*', and by the end of the War it was to be the British who possessed one-ton bombs and the means of reaching Berlin!

During the first two years of the War several German manufacturers embarked on the production of huge bombers (officially classified as *Riesen*, or Giants), colossal aircraft with three, four or even five engines and which spanned as much as the B-29 Superfortress of the Second World War. Some of these saw active service in the East, and more than a dozen of the great Zeppelin-Staaken R VIs equipped *Riesenflugzeugabteilungen 500* and *501* under Hauptmann Richard von Bentivegni near Ghent for operations in the West, including a number of raids on London.

At the same time a rather smaller class of bomber, the G-series, was being developed of which the best known and most widely used were to be the Friedrichshafen G III, and the Gotha G IV and G V. Spurred by realisation of the limitations of the airship's value as a raiding weapon, the Gotha G IV was developed, appearing towards the end of 1916. It was a twin-engined biplane whose two 260-hp water-cooled Mercedes engines were located on either side of the fuselage and drove pusher propellers; with a crew of three (occasionally four) it could carry up to 1,100 lb of bombs, its normal load being six 110-lb bombs. For defence it mounted up to three Parabellum guns in the nose and amidships. (Despite its size and load-carrying capabilities, a fully-laden G IV weighed considerably *less* than a Focke-Wulf Fw 190 fighter of 1941!)

During the spring of 1917 thirty Gotha G IVs were delivered to *Kagohl 3–Kampfgeschwader 3* of the OHL (later dubbed the '*England Geschwader*'), based at St Denis Westrem and Gontrode in Belgium under the command of Hauptmann Ernst Brandenburg; these were followed in July by 15 further aircraft, based at Mariakerke. As was customary in the German bombers, the aircraft commander was not the pilot but was responsible for the navigation and bomb aiming; Brandenburg's pilot was Oberleutnant Freiherr von Trotha.

After a difficult period of crew training Brandenburg declared himself ready to start raiding England, and on Friday May 25, 1917 23 Gothas set course for London. Flying at about 12,000 ft the German formation made landfall near Burnham-on-Crouch in Essex but, finding his path to the English capital barred by towering cloud, Brandenburg turned his bombers south over Kent, eventually arriving over Folkestone where most of the aircraft unloaded their bombs. No fewer than 95 people were killed and 260 injured–yet less than five tons of bombs had fallen. The anti-aircraft guns at Dover put up a heavy barrage but their shells burst ineffectually 4,000 ft below the raiders. More than 70 British aircraft took off in pursuit, but none caught up with the Gothas.

A second raid by 22 Gothas against the naval dockyard at Sheerness on June 5 killed 45 on the ground, and this time a single bomber was brought down by the gun defences.

Brandenburg's most destructive raid was to be the next, flown by 20 G IVs on June 13. In almost

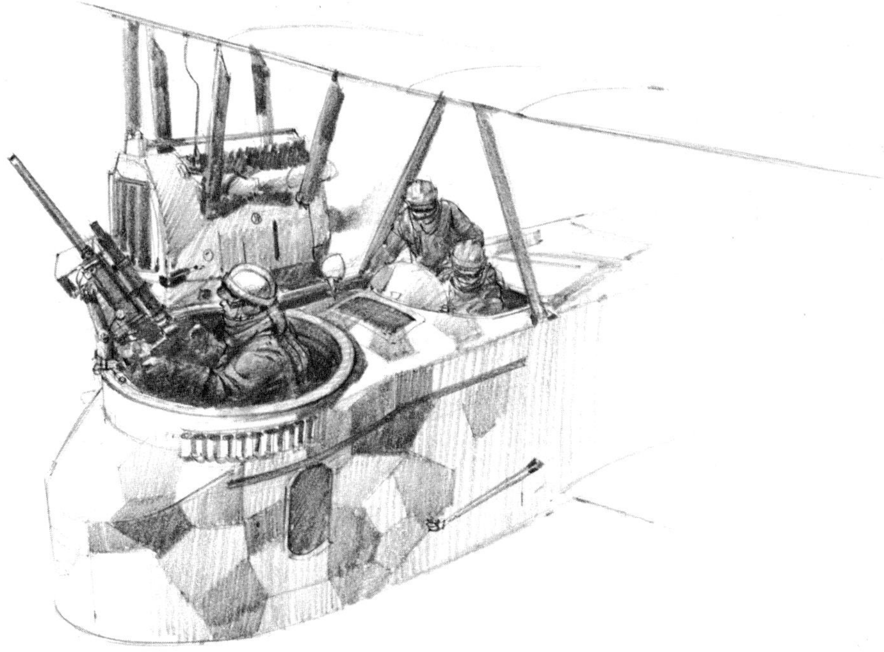

cloudless skies 14 of his crews arrived over London where their bombs struck Liverpool Street station as well as other targets in the City and dockland. A total of 162 people were killed and 432 injured. Once more the defences were helpless, and a Bristol Fighter which caught up with the bombers landed back at base with a dead gunner.

Several further raids, on Folkestone, Harwich and London followed, though by diminishing numbers of G IVs owing to landing accidents and engine failures. In the last two, flown in August, few bombers managed to penetrate beyond the coast. After Brandenburg had himself been injured in an accident, morale among the G IV crews deteriorated badly, and *Kagohl 3* transferred its operations to the hours of darkness.

Much larger than the Gothas were the four-engine Zeppelin-Staaken R VI Giants of *Riesenflugzeugab-*

A Staaken on a night raid over London being intercepted by a Bristol Figher

teilung 501 (Giant Aircraft Unit 501), commanded by Hauptmann Richard von Bentivegni, which also flew night attacks on England. Though used in smaller numbers than the G IVs and Vs, the huge Giants represented a more serious menace on account of their bomb load which could comprise a single one-ton bomb. With upwards of eight crew members the R VIs of *Rfa 501* raided England at night eleven times up to 20 May 1918 and dropped a total of 65,000 lb of bombs, yet not one of them was brought down by the British defences.

For Britain the writing on the wall was plain. The impotence of the gun defences had sparked riots in London, and the Government was under severe pressure to improve the home defence squadrons of the RFC, and the recommendations of the Smuts Committee were to bring about the unified formation of the Royal Air Force on April 1, 1918. As if to underline the efficiency of this reorganisation, *Kagohl 3*'s last attack on England on the night of May 19/20, 1918, in which 28 Gothas and Giants took part, cost the Germans the loss of six bombers–three to fighters and three to the guns. This 20 per cent loss brought to an end the bombing attacks on Britain, but the skies of Southern England would remain clear of hostile bombers for no more than 22 years.

Maid of all Work – LVG C II

One of the best 'Maids of all Work' in service with any of the warring nations in the middle period of the First World War was the LVG C II, an essentially simple two-seat, two-bay biplane of ply- and fabric-covered spruce construction, albeit of elderly vintage.

The *Luft Verkehrs Gessellschaft GmbH* (literally the Air Traffic Company) had been producing aircraft since 1911 at the Johannisthal airfield near Berlin, and in the following year the Swiss engineer Franz Schneider joined the firm and produced the unarmed B-series aircraft which entered service with the German Army shortly before the War. In one of these aeroplanes however Schneider began experiments not only with a manually operated Parabellum machine gun on a ring mounting on the rear cockpit but also a fixed forward gun equipped with interrupter gear so as to avoid striking the propeller.

As soon as it became clear in the early months of the

War that combat between opposing aeroplanes was inevitable–signalled by the increasing use of carbines and pistols–the German Military Aviation Service headquarters early in 1915 defined a new class of aeroplane, armed two-seat biplanes of more than 150 hp, to be designated C-type aircraft. LVG immediately produced its gun-armed B-type example for evaluation by the authorities but unfortunately this crashed *en route* to the Western Front in June that year when it suffered wing failure. Nevertheless Schneider quickly produced a modified aircraft, the C I –essentially a B I with strengthened airframe, 150-hp Benz engine in place of the former 100-hp Mercedes, and a ring-mounted Parabellum for the observer. This was immediately ordered into limited production and was to become the first operational German aeroplane to be given defensive armament (as distinct from the *offensive* gun of the Fokker *Eindecker* fighting scout). The C I's duties were invariably confined to observation work, it seldom being considered necessary to afford it protection by other aircraft.

However as the work of these observation aircraft came to be fully appreciated it was obvious that only a more dedicated design would suffice, and Schneider accordingly undertook a limited redesign of the C I, substituting a 160-hp Mercedes engine and further strengthening the airframe. Light racks for up to six 22-lb bombs were provided and a storage mounting for a hand-held camera incorporated in the rear cockpit. Although by no means exclusive to the LVG, only the engine's crankcase lay within the confines of the fuselage decking, its six cylinders being exposed to the elements (and the valve gear dispensing liberal quantities of oil over the heads of the crew seated close behind). The engine's exhaust manifold discharged through a raked 'chimney' which deflected the gases over the top wing. Forty gallons of fuel were carried in a cylindrical tank suspended from the top wing scarcely 12 in from the pilot's head. A water pipe led from the radiator in the top wing centresection to the front of the cylinder jacket and this, with interplane struts, fuel pipes and exhaust pipe suggested a plumber's nightmare.

The C II wrote its own little epic in the pages of history by making the first aeroplane raid on London (a *Taube* monoplane having first dropped light bombs on Paris as long ago as August 1914). On November 28, 1916 Deckoffizier Paul Brandt (pilot) and Leutnant Walther Ilges took off, probably from the Belgian coast, and managed to reach the English capital around mid-day where, after circling in the neighbourhood of Victoria station, they dropped six 22-lb bombs, wounding six people. The defences were taken completely by surprise and the intrepid airmen managed to make good their escape, only to suffer engine failure after crossing the Channel and make a successful force landing near Boulogne.

By the end of 1916 LVG C IIs were in general use all along the Western Front giving service as a light bomber with the Infantry Contact Patrol units, some aircraft being provided with a sheet of armour under

Last of the family of LVG artillery co-operation aircraft was the C VI of 1918. Here an observer takes on board a couple of light bombs which would simply be dropped overboard

their cockpits to protect the crew from the fierce small arms fire from the trenches. As the Allied air forces introduced their first generation of fighting scouts, such as the Sopwith Pup, to counter German air activity over the battlefields most C IIs (in common with other C-types in use) were given a single synchronised Spandau machine gun to redress the odds in air combat.

Many of the future German fighter aces served their combat apprenticeship in the LVG. Max Immelmann, already dead, had flown LVG Bs and Cs and had had his first taste of combat in one during June 1915, and had spoken highly of the quality of workmanship in their construction. Joseph Veltjens (later to gain 34 victories) flew C IIs for a short spell in 1916, as did Hermann Göring (22 victories), although with the arrival of the new breed of fighting scouts

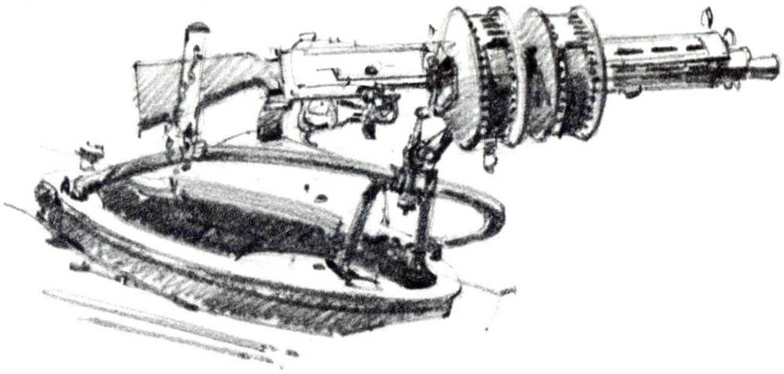

most of the aggressive young pilots could scarcely contain their impatience to obtain postings to the new *Jastas* and get their hands on the Albatros and Fokker scouts.

The Greatest Fokker – the D VII

The Fokker D VII was Germany's best fighting scout in widespread service during the final year of the War, so much so that Article IV of the Armistice document, which set out details of equipment to be sequestered by the Allies, specifically designated every surviving aircraft of this type was to be handed over–so highly was it regarded by British and French pilots.

Designed by Reinhold Platz, the D VII was universally acclaimed winner from 31 entrants in the Johannisthal competition for D-class single-seat fighting scouts held in January 1918, and was ordered into immediate production; built by both Fokker and Albatros (ironically Fokker's great rival) D VII deliveries started in April and were rushed into service on the Western Front with those *Jastas* which were operating as parts of 'circuses'–*Jagdgeschwader Nrs 1, 2* and *3*. Possessing a somewhat sinister appearance with its short blunt nose more reminiscent of Allied rather than German aircraft (the D VII was the first German operational aircraft to feature a car-type honeycomb radiator in the nose for its 160-hp Mercedes engine), the new scout was exceptionally neat and compact, utilising considerable welding in its construction: Platz himself had been a gifted welder before embarking on aircraft design.

Early aircraft at the Front were plagued by a series of accidents following engine overheating which caused the incendiary ammunition stored in the nose magazines to pre-detonate; one of those killed was Leutnant Fritz Friedrichs who, while flying with *Jasta 11*, had shot down 21 enemy aircraft. His *Pour le Mérite* had been awarded on reaching a score of 20 victories but he did not live to receive the supreme decoration. The problem was overcome by increasing the ventilation of the engine bay and introducing a new type of ammunition.

The first aircraft arrived on *Geschwader Nr 1* in mid-April at almost exactly the time of its illustrious commander's death in action; there is little doubt but that von Richthofen's personal score would have quickly accelerated even further had he laid his hands on a D VII. Before his death von Richthofen had nominated his successor as Hauptmann Wilhelm Reinhold, who had led *Jasta 6* and had been nominated for the 'Blue Max' on reaching twenty victories; Reinhold was to be killed almost immediately when the wings of an aircraft he was flying broke away during a fighter competition at Berlin. Command then passed temporarily to another famous pilot, Ernst Udet (ultimately to score 62 victories–second only to von Richthofen himself), but on July 5 Hermann Göring was officially appointed commander of *Geschwader Richthofen*, a by no means universally popular choice as, although he was an able leader, Göring's methods were very different from those of his illustrious predecessors.

D VIIs continued to replace older scouts on the *Jastas* throughout that fateful summer for Germany. After *Geschwader Nr 1's Jastas 4, 6, 10 and 11* followed *JG Nr 2*, commanded by the astonishing Rudolf Berthold–the 'Iron Knight'–who survived the War with 44 victories, many of them gained despite

MICHAEL TURNER '86

desperate wounds, only to be strangled to death in 1920 by a group of Communists who used the neck ribbon of his 'Blue Max'.

The D VII proved more than a match for such aircraft as the Sopwith Camel and the Bristol F.2B Fighter although, when flown by accomplished pilots, the excellent SE 5A possessed the edge in combat. It was largely to counter this scout and the equally good Spad S XIII that a new version, the D VIIf was developed. It was powered by a 185-hp BMW engine and capable of a speed of 125 mph. Moreover it halved the time taken to reach 16,000 ft, the height at which many combats by then took place, compared with the Mercedes-powered version. This aeroplane started to reach the *Jastas* towards the end of the summer, and was feared by the Allies in the West during the last three months of the War.

No fewer than 45 *Jastas* were flying the D VII by the autumn of 1918. As with the earlier scouts, the aircraft displayed all manner of colour schemes, although predominant colours tended to identify the *Jasta* rather than the individual pilot; it was not uncommon for some device (such as the pilot's initials or his family badge) to be painted on the side of the fuselage. Ernst Udet, for instance, carried the monogram 'LO!' in reference to his fiancé Lola Zink whom he married after the War.

The Fokker D VII represented the pinnacle of German technical achievement during the First World War. The end came as much the result of the overwhelming power of the Allied armies in France as of the Communist-inspired revolution inside Germany and the fast-debilitating scarcity of vital war supplies. In the German Air Force literally thousands of excellent aeroplanes, otherwise ready for combat, stood grounded on their airfields for want of fuel.

A Fokker D VII strafes French troops in 1918. The dedicated 'trench fighter' with downward-firing machine guns was only being developed at the very end of the First World War

Years in the Wilderness

The Armistice and the subsequent Treaty of Versailles imposed upon Germany a retribution that was at once vicious and economically crippling to an extent that displayed the former Allies' total lack of perception of the circumstances inside Germany, conditions that would inevitably nurture the very nationalistic militarism that the Treaty was intended to avoid.

While the once-proud German Navy was led away to Scapa Flow to await its ultimate fate–in the event death by its own hand–the German Air Force was thrown on the scrap heap and the aircraft industry forbidden to construct military aircraft. The architects of the Treaty had however overlooked the potential of commercial aviation and certainly failed to perceive an interrelation between commercial and military aircraft design. An unexplained and–in the context of the humbling Treaty–illogical dispensation allowed Germany to retain a defence ministry in Berlin, the *Reichswehr Ministerium*, under General Hans von Seeckt. This legitimised façade was able to assemble some of the most able German officers and as early as 1923 they secretly laid plans to create a new German Air Force, independent of the Army. Men like Kesselring, Wolfram von Richthofen (cousin of the great Manfred), Sperrle and Stumpff, all of whom were to occupy high command positions in the Luftwaffe 20 years later, served on von Seeckt's Staff. Moreover, unsuspected by the Western Powers, von Seeckt managed to negotiate with Russia for the secret training of key flying personnel at Lipetsk, south-east of Moscow.

Focke-Wulf Fw 44 Stieglitz

Another of von Seeckt's protégés was Ernst Brandenburg, wartime commander of the *England Geschwader*, who was appointed head of the German Civil Aviation Department, thereby cementing control of commercial aviation to the military authorities. Within the sphere of Brandenburg's administration was the *Deutscher Luftsportverband* (German Union of Sporting Flying), a civilian association formed in 1920 that by 1926 had grown to an active membership of 20,000, and 50,000 three years later. The policy of the association, encouraged by the defence ministry, was to motivate airmindedness through the sporting instincts of the German people.

In the absence of an indigenous aircraft industry however there were very few light sporting aeroplanes in Germany during the early 1920s (and in the appalling conditions of raging inflation they would have found precious few buyers) and attention turned to the manufacture of hundreds of elementary gliders, aircraft of great simplicity which could be stored in small sheds and garages. With adequate government financial support to encourage the formation of countless gliding clubs throughout the country, going about their legitimate recreation in full view of foreign observers, Germany could quietly claim to possess greater airmindedness than any other nation in Europe. Figures for 1927 for instance show that more

than 15,000 Germans had received their certificates in gliding proficiency – far in excess of all other European nations together. By this expedient, as well as the Lipetsk training agreement, von Seeckt circumvented the strictures of the Versailles Treaty, and developed the basis on which a future air force might be built.

Meanwhile limited commercial aviation had continued in Germany almost since the Armistice of 1918, first through the *Deutsche Luft-Reederei* which flew adaptations of ex-military aircraft, and from 1926 through Lufthansa. Not even the terms of the 1926 Paris Air Agreement, which was intended to limit the number of German military personnel permitted to fly, presented any real obstacle to the growth of flying in Germany; Lufthansa simply recruited Lipetsk-trained would-be military aircrew, gave them two or more years' flying on the air routes, and then transferred them to administrative duties.

Even when the economic depression spread throughout the Western world after October 1929, causing Lufthansa's government subsidy to be halved, German flying training continued with scarcely any slackening of enthusiasm – the gliders used no fuel! It was now that another figure from the past surfaced in German aviation circles in the portly form of Hermann Göring, a former wartime pilot of moderate distinction. Political opportunism and Prussian aristocratic influence had brought nomination as a Reichstag deputy, and it was this influence that resulted in the reinstatement of financial support for continuing military training. He went further when addressing the Reichstag in secret by openly supporting the rebirth of a German air force. Acquisition of power by the NSDAP in 1933 and Germany's walk-out from the Geneva Disarmament Conference were all that were needed – on the pretext of defence against her neighbours – to bring about that re-birth.

Heinkel He 111

THE RESURGENCE OF AIR POWER

The Luftwaffe's First Fighter – Heinkel He 51

The political upheavals that accompanied the acquisition of power by Adolf Hitler and the NSDAP in 1932-33 masked the activities of Hermann Göring who was seeking to enlist the assistance of Erhard Milch who, as head of Lufthansa, had in turn frequently sought Göring's influence to provide the means by which the German airline could survive the ravages of the great Depression. Göring respected Milch's administrative gifts, realising that as head of German commercial aviation he also possessed the means to shape the re-birth of a German air force. It was largely through the efforts of Milch, as yet politically untainted, that Germany's surviving aircraft manufacturers, some of whom had gone abroad to continue their business–but who now returned–were persuaded to embark on the production of military aircraft.

While Hitler appointed Göring Special Commissioner for Aviation it fell to Milch to set up a new Air Ministry, whose Air Staff (with such men as Kesselring, Stumpff and Wever) was charged with creating the new Luftwaffe, recruiting the personnel and ordering new aircraft–the latter task falling to Oberst Wimmer.

Already flying with Lufthansa was a generation of aircraft (the Junkers Ju 52/3m among others) capable of relatively straightforward adaptation as bombers. Other aircraft, ostensibly produced for sporting flying, were equally adaptable as trainers. More difficult–indeed more pressing–was the provision of fighters, a type of aeroplane which had been expressly forbidden to Germany for 15 years and therefore one in which the aircraft designers possessed little modern experience. Based purely on the proven capabilities of the best of foreign fighters, the first tentative specifications were issued to the industry before the end of 1933.

Meanwhile Ernst Heinkel, who had formed his own company in December 1922 for the purpose of producing aircraft for the Swedish SAAB company, had opened a new factory at Rostock in 1932. It was to be his company that won a contract to produce the

The scene could be Tangmere in England in the mid-1930s, but these attractive biplane fighters are the new Luftwaffe's Heinkel He 51s, the men future pilots of the Emil

Luftwaffe's first operational fighter, the attractive Heinkel He 51, whose performance specification was based on the latest versions of the British Hawker Fury. Of typical 'early 1930s' appearance, the He 51 was a single-bay biplane with spatted undercarriage and twin-gun armament. After trials in 1934 it entered service with the first *Jagdgeschwader* in April 1935, and soon afterwards joined the three 'Publicity Squadrons', formed to encourage recruitment. A twin-float version, the He 51B-2, also equipped *Küstenjagdgruppe 136*, a coastal fighter group.

Wimmer's plans called for the production of some 120 He 51s by the end of 1935 and by the summer of 1936 the aircraft represented the most widely-used interceptor in the Luftwaffe. Most famous of the units equipped with the aircraft was JG 132 <*Richthofen*> whose task, although listed as an operational Wing, was to provide fighter training for the most promising of Germany's fledgling pilots. In 1936, with the introduction of the Arado Ar 68 fighter, attention turned to use of the He 51 as a ground attack fighter, and the aircraft began appearing on the *Stukageschwader* (*Stuka* being a contraction of *Sturzkampfflugzeug*, or dive bomber). One of these Wings, St.G 165 at Kitzingen, received He 51A-1s equipped to carry six 22-lb fragmentation bombs and set about training in the task of ground support. Among the pilots who flew with this unit was a 25-year-old NCO pilot, Robert Olejnik, later to take a leading part in development flying of the Luftwaffe's Messerschmitt Me 163 rocket fighter and gain a Knight's Cross as a fighter ace with 32 victories in the Second World War.

It was the work done by St.G 165 that resulted in the He 51 being sent to serve with the Condor Legion in the Spanish Civil War in support of Franco's Nationalist forces. Among the great names to emerge from that tragic war was that of Adolf Galland, a beneficiary of the old gliding craze prior to the Luftwaffe's re-birth, who accompanied volunteers to Spain abroad a *Kraft durch Freude* (Strength Through Joy) tourist liner. Arriving in May 1937 Galland was posted to the Northern Front where he was given command of *3.Staffel*, *Jagdverband 88*, equipped with He 51s. Already however this aircraft had shown itself to be outclassed in combat with the Republican-flown Russian I-15s, so that the *3.Staffel* was ordered to fly low and avoid air combat. Nevertheless the work Galland did, 'ground-strafing the Rojos', provided vital experience in the task of supporting the forces on the ground – a task already seen to be the *raison d'être* of the Luftwaffe in the years to come.

By 1937 the He 51's days as an operational fighter were over. Already Willy Messerschmitt's superb Bf 109 monoplane had flown and pointed the way ahead. Thereafter the biplane was relegated to fighter training with the *Jagdfliegerschulen*, He 51s with the Magdeburg and Schleissheim schools continuing in service well into the Second World War.

Falcons and Fledglings – Focke-Wulf Fw 56 Stösser

Formed at Bremen in 1924 by Prof Heinrich Focke, Georg Wulf and Dr Werner Neumann to produce single-engine commercial transport aircraft, the Focke-Wulf Flugzeugbau AG amalgamated with the old *Albatros Flugzeugwerke GmbH* in September 1931, securing the services of Dipl Ing Kurt Tank as chief designer two months later.

The first aircraft in which Tank was fully involved was a parasol monoplane, the Fw 56, to which the designer – perpetuating Focke's tradition of giving birds' names to his aircraft – applied the name *Stösser* (Falcon). Despite the parasol wing arrangement and curious 'tailplane on fin' layout, the *Stösser* proved a delight to fly, being highly manoeuvrable and surprisingly robust. When the formation of the Luftwaffe became a reality, and with it the need for an advanced training aircraft, the Fw 56, which first flew in November 1933, was an obvious choice. The following year, with the issue of the first formal Service specifications, the first two pre-production aircraft were armed with a pair of synchronised MG 17 machine guns in the upper fuselage decking, as well as racks for three 22-lb practice bombs. In this configuration the *Stösser* was entered in a *Reichsluftfahrtministerium* (RLM, the Air Ministry) competition to select a light home defence fighter/trainer and, beating the He 74 and Ar 76, was ordered into quantity production. As a means of concealing the full and growing strength of the Luftwaffe from foreign observers more than 400 Fw 56s were delivered to countless civil flying clubs throughout Germany, many Service pilots receiving their final operational training from civilian instructors (themselves Luftwaffe 'reservists').

Meanwhile that superb pilot, Ernst Udet, who was welcomed throughout the flying world, had recently returned from a trip to the United States where he had been particularly impressed by a demonstration of a Curtiss Helldiver dive bomber. Now an ardent

Kurt Tank's Stösser *narrowly missed serving as a dive bomber, instead being 'relegated' to the training rôle; nevertheless as such it was among the best trainers in Europe*

The Heinkel He 51 was outlived by its contemporary Bücker Bü 133 Jungmeister

advocate of dive-bombing tactics by the Luftwaffe in its intended rôle as air support arm of the Wehrmacht (German Army), Udet obtained a *Stösser* with which to experiment in dive-bombing attacks against a target set up on Bremen airfield. Carrying small concrete-filled bombs on makeshift racks he was able to demonstrate much improved bombing accuracy with these tactics compared with level bombing from medium altitude, particularly in the confined space of a congested battlefield. A year later Udet was appointed to lead the RLM's technical department, and he it was who demonstrated the Ju 87 in similar tactics to such good effect that the dive bomber became officially accepted by the Luftwaffe.

Powered by no more than a 240-hp Argus eight-cylinder air-cooled in-line engine, the *Stösser* possessed a speed of just over 170 mph, a creditable performance almost exactly comparable with that of the RAF's standard but aged two-gun interceptor, the Bristol Bulldog, with more than twice the power.

Among the earliest units to fly the *Stösser* was the *Jagdfliegerschule* at Schleissheim in 1935, and by the outbreak of the Second World War it was serving with a number of other fighter schools, including A/B 41 at Frankfurt-an-der-Oder on the German border with Poland, and later with A/B 112 at Langenlebarn. With the formation in the later stages of the War of 'fighter-conversion Wings' to re-employ ex-bomber pilots on interceptor duties over the Reich the *Stösser*, of which about 1,000 had by then been built, was considered the ideal 'forgiving' trainer to introduce experienced bomber and other pilots to fighter tactics, and such units as JG 101 at Zerbst near Magdeburg employed Fw 56s in 1943, as did JG 108 at Bad Vöslau the following year.

One of many pilots who struck up a lasting affinity with the *Stösser* was the 27-year-old Major Heinrich Ehrler who, as *Kommodore* of *Jagdgeschwader 5*, acquired one of these aeroplanes for his personal use in 1944. Ehrler, who as local fighter commander in Norway was court-martialled after the sinking of the battleship *Tirpitz* but was acquitted, shot down 204 Russian aircraft during the War and was a holder of the Oakleaves to the Knight's Cross (having been nominated for the Swords when hostilities ended).

Trouble with Diesels – Junkers Ju 86

The somewhat nebulous Junkers Ju 86, designed and developed under the leadership of Dipl Ing Ernst Zindel, was the outcome of discussions between Erhard Milch and the Junkers company early in 1933. Unlike however the Junkers Ju 52/3m, which had already flown in commercial transport form the previous year and whose adaptation as a 'bomber-transport' was already envisaged for the yet-unborn Luftwaffe, the Ju 86 was in fact conceived from the outset as an aircraft of which two dedicated versions, one a bomber and the other an airliner, would be developed in parallel. Milch indeed made it clear to Junkers that the 10-seat commercial version must lose nothing by compromise with the bomber. As it transpired however it was to be the bomber to which priority was given, although the choice of diesel engines did more to compromise both versions than anything else. The requirement by both civil and military authorities (*sic*) called for a top speed of 350 km/h (218 mph), but when powered by the Jumo 205 'heavy oil' engines the early Ju 86s could manage no more than about 190 mph.

The first military Ju 86 made its maiden flight on November 4, 1934 (the first commercial prototype being flown in April 1935). From all accounts these early examples were thoroughly unpleasant to fly, exhibiting sluggish control characteristics and frightening instability at low speed. The unusual undercarriage whose main units, hinged at the wing roots, retracted *outwards* into the wings *inboard* of the engine nacelles, and was therefore of exceptionally narrow track and gave rise to very tricky landing characteris-

If the Second World War had started in 1938 the Ju 86, seen here during 1937 exercises, would have provided much of the Luftwaffe's bombing power – despite continuing engine problems

tics to say the least–not by any means improved by poor directional stability in the landing condition with the full-span auxiliary wing flaps extended.

While production went ahead with exports to Sweden, Switzerland, Hungary, Portugal, Chile and South Africa (most nations opted to specify conventional petrol engines), the Luftwaffe decided to persevere with the Jumo diesels despite appalling unserviceability. By the end of 1935 manufacture of the first pre-production Ju 86A-0s was underway and these were evaluated by RLM pilots early the following year, about a dozen A-1s then joining *Kampfgeschwader 152* <*Hindenburg*>, to serve alongside the Luftwaffe's first Ju 52/3ms in the bomber rôle. KG 152 was the first dedicated bomber Geschwader in the new Luftwaffe; in 1937 the Ju 52/3ms were transferred away from the 'pure' bomber units, their place being taken by Heinkel He 111s.

The Ju 86 carried a crew of four or five, two gunners manning machine guns in a dorsal position and a retractable ventral 'dustbin'–a curious but surprisingly widely adopted defence expedient among British, French and German bombers of the mid-1930s.

The next military version was the Ju 86D-1 which entered Luftwaffe service in 1936, featuring a small dorsal fin extending to the extreme tail (first introduced on the commercial Ju 86C) to improve the lateral stability; in fact the benefit was only marginal. Five Ju 86D-1s were sent to Spain with the Condor Legion during the autumn of 1937 but these proved hopeless under operational conditions owing to engine unserviceability, seldom more than two aircraft ever being available simultaneously.

Realisation had however dawned that the diesel engines were simply not worth the trouble and at

home in Germany during the summer of 1937 the first Ju 86E-1s with conventional 810-hp BMW radial engines entered service, followed by E-2s with power increased to 865-hp. The Ju 86G, with a redesigned nose intended to improve the pilot's field of view, was introduced in 1938.

Although continuing disappointment with the Ju 86 and the introduction of the greatly superior Heinkel He 111 bomber caused the Junkers aircraft to be relegated to bomber training in 1939, it was not the end of the Ju 86 as an operational aircraft, nor of the diesel engine. Following considerable research by Junkers in high altitude flight, which dated back to 1931, a new version of the aircraft, the Ju 86P with 950-hp Jumo 207A diesels and a pressure cabin for its two-man crew, was flown in 1940 and delivered to the secret *Aufklärungsgruppe Oberbefehlshaber der Luftwaffe* (literally, the Luftwaffe C-in-C's Reconnaissance Group), led by Oberstleutnant Theodor Rowehl. Flying at almost 40,000 ft, these aircraft flew a number of sorties over England during that memorable summer–without any interference possible from RAF Fighter Command. Later in the War further development with improved engines and extended wings enabled the Ju 86P (and Ju 86R) to attain heights approaching 50,000 ft. Their ability to reach such great altitudes was bought at the expense of armament. These aircraft were particularly active over the Mediterranean, as well as Britain and the Eastern Front, and although the RAF was to introduce special Spitfires and Mosquitos to counter the menace, successful interceptions were rare.

The First Dive Bombers – Henschel Hs 123

Germany's attractive Henschel Hs 123 was one of that anachronistic trio of biplanes (the others being the British Gloster Gladiator and the Italian Fiat CR.42 *Falco*) that was born into a world fast becoming dominated by monoplanes, yet survived to perform with worthwhile distinction long into the Second World War. But whereas the other two were interceptor fighters, the Hs 123 was a ground attack/close support aircraft.

First flown early in 1935 the Hs 123 was the outcome of a requirement formulated in 1933 by Ernst Udet, an ardent protagonist of dive bombing principles, for a single-seat biplane capable of a speed of about 200 mph and of carrying up to 550 lb of bombs which would be delivered in diving attacks. Two contenders to this requirement, the Hs 123 and the Fieseler Fi 98, were produced but the latter, with its plethora of struts, was discarded in favour of the extraordinarily neat, clean and compact Henschel design. Of sesquiplane configuration, it featured single streamlined interplane struts and a large cantilever, faired undercarriage with wheel spats. The pilot's cockpit, located well aft of the wings, was afforded an excellent field of view for its occupant.

All did not go well to begin with, two of the first three prototypes being lost during diving trials when their top wings parted company from the aircraft, resulting in much strengthening of the attachment struts on the fourth example. Production got under way in 1936 and the first Hs 123A-1s emerged from the factories at Johannisthal and Schönefeld that summer. Powered by 880-hp BMW radial engines and capable of carrying a 550-lb bomb under the fuselage and four 110-lb bombs under the wings, these aircraft joined the experimental dive-dombing establishment at Schwerin in October, and two months later five examples were sent to Spain with the Condor Legion.

In the meantime some reappraisal of the close support tactics to be adopted by the Luftwaffe had resulted in a redefinition of the Henschel's rôle. Surviving records suggest that Udet, now head of the RLM's technical department, was less than satisfied with the aircraft's performance as a dive bomber (despite it far exceeding the original requirement), while the Ju 87 monoplane, which had been flying for more than a year, seemed ideally suited to diving attacks. Early in 1937 several new line units came into existence; the Schwerin unit became *I.Gruppe, Stukageschwader 162* and was soon to be joined by a second Gruppe to constitute the *Immelmann-Geschwader*; I./St.G 162 gave up its Hs 123s in favour of the Ju 87, and by the summer they only equipped *Stukageschwader 165*, and the Condor Legion in Spain.

It was to be in Spain that the Henschel's true role was evolved. Forbidden to venture above about 1,000 ft to avoid combat with the nimble I-15 fighters of the Republican forces, the pilots of the Hs 123 *Kette* soon become extremely efficient in their sweeps over the opposing ground forces, using their light bombs sparingly but effectively against small concentrations of troops and vehicles, and shooting up targets of opportunity with their twin synchronised MG 17

Henschel Hs 123s, in Condor Legion colours, dive bombing in Spain; excellent though they were, they soon took second place to the much vaunted Junkers Ju 87 – the Stuka

machine guns. Thus for a short time in 1938 a newly-styled type of unit, the *Schlachtfliegergruppe* (Assault Flying Group) came into being, two of these, SFG 10 and SFG 50, being equipped with Hs 123s.

By the date of Germany's attack on Poland, September 1, 1939, only one operational unit still flew the aircraft, II. (Schlacht)/LG 2, commanded by Major Werner Spielvogel. Flying from Alt-Rosenburg the 'one-two-threes' operated in support of the German XIV Army in its advance on Warsaw. Due to its relatively light armament the biplane was unable to inflict much material damage, yet the booming roar of its BMW engine was enough to stampede the Polish Army's horses and strike fear and confusion among the poorly organised troops confronting the mighty Wehrmacht.

Spielvogel was to be killed in the Polish campaign, his place being taken by Otto Weiss, the man largely responsible for the continuing success of the old biplane. The award of the Knight's Cross to Weiss on May 18, 1940, in respect of his brilliant leadership of II./LG 2 in the Battle of France, was one of the first two such awards made to the Luftwaffe during the War (the other being to Generalmajor Wolfram, Freiherr von Richthofen, former commander of the Condor Legion, an ardent advocate of the dive bomber and, in 1940, commander of *VIII (Schlacht) Fliegerkorps*). In the Battle of France II./LG 2's Hs 123s were involved in clearing the way for the German armour across the Albert Canal.

Although production ended in 1940, Hs 123s continued in service with II./LG 2 until early in 1942 when the unit was disbanded to provide the nucleus of *Schlachtgeschwader 1*, a new assault unit flying Hs 123s, Hs 129s and its own fighter protection of Bf 109s. So successful were the 'old assaulters' that von Richthofen demanded in January 1943 that the Hs 123 be put back into production (this proved impractical as the old jigs had been scrapped). In all, II./LG 2 and Sch.G 1 produced no fewer than 42 holders of the Knight's Cross, of whom 27 flew the old biplane—which continued to serve operationally until mid-1944—a truly extraordinary testimony to great human courage and an excellent aeroplane.

Modern Bombers over Spain – Heinkel He 111

When first conceived in 1934 the Heinkel He 111, designed by Siegfried and Walter Gunter, was undoubtedly the most advanced military aircraft in the world, its performance being at least comparable with the best interceptor fighters. Yet such was the tremendous pace of technology in the final years of peace it was to become obsolescent by international standards within eight years.

Like the Junkers Ju 86, the He 111 was to be developed simultaneously as a 'medium' bomber and as a high-speed commercial airliner. First flight by the military prototype was undertaken at Rostock by Flugkapitän Gerhard Nitschke on February 24, 1935, followed three weeks later by the commercial prototype. Possessing graceful elliptical wings and tail surfaces, the early He 111s featured a beautifully streamlined fuselage marred only by the orthodox stepped cockpit windscreen.

It was fairly clear that the original specification had not however been fully thought out for, although early pre-production He 111A-0s, with 660-hp BMW engines, achieved about 200 mph without military load their speed fell to little more than 120 mph when weighted down by bombs, fuel and four-man crew; moreover in such configuration they proved most reluctant to take off!

Nevertheless, while RLM pilots were criticising the He 111As on these scores, Heinkel was already

Early Heinkel He 111s in Spain. The 220-lb bombs were stored vertically in the aircraft's bomb bay, hence the seemingly untidy 'tumbling' effect as the bomber releases its load

25
24
25
28
MICHAEL TURNER

working to improve performance, reducing the wing span and fitting progressively more powerful engines. The He 111B-1 was powered by 880-hp Daimler Benz and, anxious to test its new aircraft in operational conditions, the Luftwaffe sent 30 of them to Spain to serve with *Kampfgruppe 88* of the Condor Legion in February 1937. Armed with three defensive MG 15 machine guns (including one in a retractable ventral 'dustbin') and capable of carrying 2,200 lb of bombs internally at a speed of around 200 mph, K/88's Heinkels flew their first raid on March 9 when they bombed the Republican airfields at Madrid-Barajas and Alcala. In subsequent raids, when the Government fighters attempted to interfere, the Heinkels were invariably able to make good their escape by virtue of their high speed.

By mid-1937 production of He 111Bs was in full swing at both Marienehe and Oranienburg, and the B-2 with 950-hp DB engines replaced the B-1; in September the later version arrived in Spain where it equipped a new Staffel at the north coastal airfield of Llanes. By then the Heinkels had virtually replaced the Ju 52/3ms in the bombing rôle, while the Ju 86s contributed scarcely anything.

Meanwhile in Germany development of the new bomber was going ahead at full speed. It had already become obvious that engine development would have to be speeded up if the full potential of the new generation of military aircraft was to be exploited–during the 'wilderness years' Germany had frequently purchased engines from abroad for her commercial aircraft; now that an air force was in the process of overt creation, foreign manufacturers were becoming increasingly reluctant to sell their modern technology. Thus it was that Junkers, BMW and Daimler Benz produced a host of engines, some of which were less than successful but all representing steady progress towards parity in performance and reliability with the best British, American and French engines.

By the end of 1937 the Luftwaffe possessed a fully operational bomber force with the formation of District Commands. The first *Geschwader* to receive the B-1 had been *KG 154* <*Boelcke*> at Hannover-Langenhagen in 1936, later to be redesignated *KG 157*; this was joined by *KG 152* <*Hindenburg*>, *KG 155*, *KG 253* <*General Wever*>, *KG 257* and *KG 355*. At the beginning of 1938 the next major production version, the He 111E, started to appear. This version had a pair of 1,000-hp Jumo 211 engines which increased the top speed to no less than 260 mph, despite the retention of the 'dustbin'. Among the first to appear was a batch sent to Spain in January which served initially at El Burgo de Osma in Soria.

By all accounts the pre-War Heinkels were popular among their crews, their fine performance supporting a very definite élitist standing within the Luftwaffe. After the death of General Wever, the first Chief of Air Staff, in a flying accident in 1936, all serious attempts to create a truly strategic bombing force were abandoned. Wever, who pictured the Luftwaffe as a balanced, independent air force, had advocated the creation of such a force capable of reaching every corner of Europe from bases in Germany, lending support to such aircraft as the four-engine Dornier Do 19 and Junkers Ju 89; the former was abandoned and the latter became a transport. Wever was succeeded by Albert Kesselring who, with Hitler and Göring, demanded a much bigger force of smaller aircraft, and it was the He 111 that was to benefit most from this philosophy. It was generally considered that one could build three He 111s for every Ju 89, and Hitler was much more interested in a bomber force of three hundred aircraft than one of one hundred, while Göring remarked that three bomb aimers were better than one!

First Taste of Blitzkrieg – Junkers Ju 87

The arrival of the Junkers Ju 87 in the Luftwaffe's arsenal in 1937 probably did more than anything else to alert the world to the growing danger that Germany's air force represented, for here was an attack weapon conceived for aggression–with no possible motivation for defence. The sinister, angular aeroplane with weirdly cranked wings and large bomb carried externally only heightened its purposeful appearance. There is no doubt but that the Luftwaffe did envisage the Stuka as an offensive weapon, not only capable of great bombing accuracy but to be flown in a manner intended to terrorise and confuse enemy forces on the ground. As such it was a key weapon of the Wehrmacht's devastating Blitzkrieg tactic.

With such influential advocates as Udet and Kesselring (Wolfram von Richthofen was not wholly convinced until 1938), the progress of the Ju 87 into service was swift. First flown in the spring of 1935 with a Rolls-Royce Kestrel engine, it was selected in preference to the Arado Ar 81, Blohm und Voss Ha 137 and Heinkel He 118 after competitive trials at Rechlin early the following year (Udet crashed the Heinkel but escaped injury).

Early in 1937 the first production Ju 87A-1s with 635-hp Jumo 210 engines and large, fixed undercarriage 'trousers', were delivered to *I./St.G 162* *<Immelmann>* (soon re-designated St.G 163) at Schwerin, this unit being tasked with evolving operational dive bombing tactics. Quickly earning the nickname *Jolanthe* (after a popular theatrical pig), three Ju 87As were sent to Spain for service with the Condor Legion where they constituted the *Jolanthe-Kette*. These three aircraft went into action in the mountainous area round Teruel, north-west of Valencia, later supporting the Nationalists' drive to the Mediterranean coast; they also participated in the offensive in Catalonia as well as the fighting on the Ebro front. These Ju 87As were remarkably effective, always being regarded with trepidation by the Republicans. Their crews seldom spent more than three or four months in Spain before rotating with others from Germany so as to afford the largest number of pilots and gunner/wireless operators experience in combat conditions.

The excellent and reliable service provided by this *Kette* finally convinced General Freiherr von Richthofen, Chief of Staff of the Condor Legion between November 1938 and May 1939, of the value of the dive bomber as a precision weapon on the field of battle. At his request five of the much-improved Ju 87B-1s were sent to Spain with 900-hp Jumo 211 engines, redesigned cockpit enclosures, enlarged tail surfaces, 'spatted' landing gear with *Jericho-Trompeten* ('Trumpets of Jericho' sirens), and capable of carrying a 1,100-lb bomb under the fuselage. Forming a new *Staffel* these aircraft were frequently employed in raids on the Spanish ports of Barcelona, Tarragona and Valencia in 1939, sinking and damaging a large number of Republican ships (bringing war matériel from communist sympathisers abroad) and devastating the dock facilities. There is no doubt that the large number of civilians who died only served to fuel the international outcry that denigrated the German 'terror raids'. Be that as it may, the legend of the Stuka was born in the Spanish war–a war that provided priceless experience for an air force that was scarcely five years old.

Back in Germany the *Stukaverband* was growing rapidly, with many of the most experienced and influential pilots in the fledgling air force gaining preferential selection to the new élite units. Indeed a number of officer members of the aristocracy chose to re-muster from the Army to the Luftwaffe, being persuaded by Göring that greater prestige would attach to the Stuka and *Zerstörerverbande*. Such men as Robert-Georg Freiherr von Malapert-Neufville (*St.G 165*), Friedrich-Karl Freiherr von Dalwigk zu Lichtenfels (*St.G 162*, later to be killed in the Battle of Britain) and Clemens Graf von Schönborn-Wiesentheid (*St.G 165*) were prominent among the original line pilots who flew Ju 87s before the War. Among the pilots who served on *I./St.G 163* at Breslau in 1938 was a 24-year-old Leutnant, Friedrich Lang, who would one day receive both the Swords and Oakleaves to the Knight's Cross, and would remain with the unit throughout the Second World War; *I./St.G 163* was to be redesignated *St.G 2* *<Immelmann>* before the War.

Training of the Stuka units did not go entirely smoothly. *I./St.G 168* was re-designated *I./St.G 76* shortly before the Second World War and was tasked to spearhead the assault on Poland. To carry out rehearsals for this attack the Gruppe, based at Graz in Austria (hence being dubbed the '*Grazer Gruppe*'), was ordered to fly bombing sorties over the Neuhammer

29 2
29 4
MICHAEL TURNER
85

Left: *Junkers Ju 87As of the* Jolanthe Kette *(note the pig insignia on the wheel fairings); the 'splinter' camouflage, tried in Spain, was to become a familiar feature of Luftwaffe aircraft thereafter*

training area in the Sagan Heide; on a famous occasion, August 15, 1939, as the Gruppe was committed to a diving attack, a sudden convection fog enveloped the target causing no fewer than thirteen Ju 87s to dive into the ground with the loss of all crews. One of the Gruppe's survivors on this occasion was Oberleutnant Dietrich Peltz, 25-year-old *Kapitän* of *1.Staffel*; within four years this young man had been promoted to become the Luftwaffe's youngest general, and had been awarded the Swords and Oakleaves to the Knight's Cross.

Europe Suffers the Stuka – Junkers Ju 87

The first airman to fly into action in the Second World War was the 26-year-old Oberleutnant Bruno Dilley. He led his Junkers Ju 87B-equipped *3.Staffel, St.G 1* into a pinpoint dive bombing attack on Polish army positions near the Vistula bridges at Dirschau 15 minutes before 'X'-hour–the moment when Germany's forces burst across her eastern border on September 1, 1939–to prevent their demolition.

That first short campaign, which brought Poland to collapse inside a month, involved all nine of the Luftwaffe's *Stukagruppen*–all with Ju 87s–in wide-ranging attacks, not only in direct support of the swiftly advancing Wehrmacht but also further afield to destroy Polish aircraft on their airfields and troop concentrations well behind the front.

The next nine months were a period of terror for Northern Europe as the German Blitzkrieg swept through Denmark, Norway, Holland, Belgium, Luxembourg and France, each nation ill-prepared to resist the horror of total war. Almost everywhere the pattern was the same: overwhelming strength of men, guns and armour, bursting through hurriedly contrived defences where the German bombers had blasted a path. In Norway, an awkward theatre of mountains, fjords and long sea communications, the Luftwaffe was less able to employ its power to the full; yet once more the Stuka was there in the form of a long-range version, the Ju 87R, with long-range fuel tanks under the wings.

For Hitler's great assault in the West in May 1940 the Luftwaffe once more assembled nine *Stukagruppen*, the majority of them operating under Generalfeldmarschall Wolfram von Richthofen's *VIII.Fliegerkorps* in support of Guderian's Panzers. Göring boasted that his Luftwaffe would destroy the British Expeditionary Force, struggling to evacuate from the beaches of Dunkirk, but there the vaunted Stuka suffered heavily

Following pages: *bombing Piraeus harbour. Stuka observer's view of a raid on the Greek port by Hauptmann Helmut Bode's III.Gruppe, St.G 77, during the campaign of April 1941*

at the hands of RAF pilots. The battles that raged over the weary soldiers massed on those bloody beaches were but a foretaste of worse to follow.

One month's respite followed for Britain, during which the Luftwaffe began assembling on the airfields of Northern France for the great assault across the Channel. At first only six *Stukagruppen* were available, but these were soon joined by four more after the final collapse of France, so that some 340 dive bombers of *Stukageschwader 1*, *2* and *77* and *IV./LG 2* crowded the airfields in the Pas de Calais and at Caen, Angers, Lannion, Nantes, St Malo, Tramecourt and elsewhere. Possessing only limited range, the Ju 87s were to be used only along England's South Coast, in effect as long range artillery to soften up the defences prior to the great invasion.

July was a month of sporadic skirmishing in which the Stukas were committed sparingly; an attack on Portland on the 4th sank the 5,000-ton naval anti-aircraft auxiliary, HMS *Foyle Bank*, and on the 20th an attack by about 40 Ju 87s of Hauptmann Anton Keil's *II./St.G 1* on a Channel convoy cost the loss of two Stukas to the guns of RAF Hurricanes.

The dive bombers' moment of truth arrived on 8 August with the launching of widespread attacks in preparation for the invasion. On that day two raids by 57 and 82 Ju 87s, heavily escorted by fighters, attempted to attack a Channel convoy but ran into squadrons of Spitfires and Hurricanes whose pilots broke through the screens of Messerschmitts and attacked the dive bombers as they started their dives. Ten Stukas were shot down and seven damaged; two *Staffelkapitäne* were among the men lost. While recrimination followed to discover why the escorts had failed to protect their charges preparations followed for further raids. On the 13th Hauptmann von Brauchitsch's *IV.(Stuka)/LG 2* Ju 87s carried out a devastating raid on Detling airfield, killing 67 personnel (including the Station Commander) and destroying 22 aircraft, all without loss. Further west however *St.G 2* and *St.G 77* ran into Spitfires over Lyme Bay and lost six aircraft. The next day LG 2 lost four, and two more on the 15th. On the 16th the RAF fighter airfield at Tangmere suffered a deluge of bombs from two *Gruppen* of *St.G 2* but these in turn were heavily attacked by RAF pilots who shot down 11 Ju 87s and damaged five others. It was St.G 77's turn once more on the 18th when 85 Stukas attacked airfields and radar stations on the South Coast but found Spitfires and Hurricanes awaiting them. Eighteen Ju 87s were shot down, taking with them three more *Staffelkapitäne*; nine other Stukas were damaged.

Ten days' fighting had cost the *Stukaverbande* the loss of 60 aircraft and more than 130 aircrew killed, missing or taken prisoner. With some 50 other aircraft damaged more or less seriously, the Stuka force had lost about one-third of its effective strength, and the invasion had not yet been launched. The lesson was being learned: the dreaded dive bomber was fatally vulnerable in the presence of modern single-seat interceptors. Little wonder therefore that Göring decided to withdraw his Ju 87s from all but limited use in the Battle of Britain.

Stukas Versus the Red Army – Junkers Ju 87

Despite the bloody nose received over England's South Coast in August 1940 the Junkers Ju 87 returned to the fight once more when the Luftwaffe was called on to prop up Mussolini's struggling forces in the Mediterranean and Balkans in 1941. In January that year *I./St.G 1* under Hauptmann Paul-Werner Hozzel and *II./St.G 2* commanded by Major Walter Enneccerus landed at Trapani in Sicily to lend weight to attacks on British shipping in the Central Mediterranean and to neutralise the Royal Navy's vital island base of Malta. On the 10th the two *Gruppen* attacked and severely crippled the carrier HMS *Illustrious*, and a few days later hit her again in Valletta harbour. Enneccerus, who had won the Knight's Cross for his exploits in the Polish and French campaigns, was to gain an outstanding reputation for attacks on Allied ships, sinking the cruiser HMS *Southampton* on January 11 and damaging the carrier HMS *Formidable* on May 25 that year.

In the Greek campaign *St.G 2* under the 40-year-old 'Uncle' Oskar Dinort–who had been taught to fly at Lipetsk in the 1920s–took a prominent part, performing all the successful tactics of Blitzkrieg where the inept efforts by Italy's *Regia Aeronautica* had patently failed. A month later, in May 1941, *St.G 2* sank the cruiser HMS *Gloucester* and a number of destroyers during the invasion of Crete. By then however, despite being capable of carrying a 2,200-lb bomb, the Ju 87B was regarded as far too vulnerable for operation in the presence of recently-introduced Allied fighters (such as the Hurricane II and P-40 Tomahawk), and production was under way of a much beefed-up version, the Ju 87D with increased armour protection, a 1,400-hp Jumo 211J engine and capable of mounting a 4,000-lb bomb under the fuselage as well as a 1,100-lb bomb under each wing.

Although not ready for combat service when Hitler unleashed his Wehrmacht against the Soviet Union (Operation Barbarossa) on June 22, 1941, the Ju 87D began to replace the B-version before the end of that

Junkers Ju 87Ds of Oberstleutnant Walter Sigel's Stukageschwader 3 *in the Western Desert. Their white fuselage bands were a theatre marking denoting African service*

year. In February 1942 Ju 87Ds joined Hozzel's *I./St.G 2*, by then on the Leningrad Front (having moved from the Mediterranean). Two months later the first desert-equipped version was delivered to *St.G 3* in Libya, commanded by the Lufthansa-trained Oberst Walter Sigel, another survivor of the pre-War Neuhammer disaster. This *Geschwader* was to play a prominent part in the attack on Bir Hakim, the desert position that, held by Free French forces, so delayed Rommel's advance towards El Alamein. Indeed *St.G 3* was heavily committed in the great Battle of Alamein, but suffered considerable losses both then and during the subsequent retreat to Tunis, Allied fighter superiority being so overwhelming as to prevent the Luftwaffe's dwindling fighter resources from providing adequate protection for the slow dive bombers.

In truth the Ju 87's days as a dive bomber came to an end in 1942. Already versions of the Ju 87D were being introduced without the dive brakes attached to the undersurfaces of the wings. Henceforth much greater emphasis would be placed on low level ground support both in the Mediterranean and on the Russian Front. In November 1942 a new name leapt to prominence among the *Stukaverbande* when the 26-year-old son of a Silesian priest was appointed *Staffelkapitän* of *1.Staffel* in Hozzel's *St.G 2*; Hans-Ulrich Rudel, who had already distinguished himself with the *Geschwader's III.Gruppe* when he sank the old Russian battleship *Marat* in Kronstadt harbour in September 1941 (for which he received the Knight's Cross), went on to pursue a combat career seldom, if ever, matched by any other ground attack pilot. Rudel soon acquired a new version of the Ju 87, the dedicated anti-tank Ju 87G with a pair of 40-mm guns under the wings. During the desperate fighting over the Kuban bridgehead he personally destroyed or sank no fewer than 70 Soviet landing craft in a period of just over three weeks; in July 1943, in action against Russian T 34 tanks for the first time near Kharkov, he destroyed 12 on the first day. In September he assumed command of *III./St.G 2 <Immelmann>*, having been awarded the Oakleaves as the first Stuka pilot to fly 1,000 combat sorties. On October 30 he received the Swords when his score stood at 100 enemy tanks destroyed. And so his remarkable list of achievements grew. The last eighteen months of the War were punctuated by wounds and short visits to hospital. In due course he was appointed to command the newly redesignated *Schlachtgeschwader 2* and, still flying the Ju 87G, eventually destroyed 519 tanks (as well as more than 800 other vehicles and much more besides). After receiving the Diamonds–hitherto the highest German award for bravery–Hitler bestowed on him the Golden Oakleaves, the only such award ever made. He had survived being shot down no fewer than 30 times and was wounded on five occasions (flying for more than a month after his right foot had been amputated in February 1945). When the War ended Rudel had flown a total of 2,530 combat sorties.

Apart from use by such specialist units as that led by Rudel, the Ju 87 had been withdrawn from daylight operations early in 1944, it then being flown on night harassing sorties while high-performance fighter-bombers, such as the Focke-Wulf Fw 190, took over the daylight ground attack rôle. Yet the Stuka, with its near-vertical dive, screaming sirens and devastating salvo of bombs, will be forever remembered as the deeply etched symbol of Germany's crushing Blitzkrieg as, relentlessly, the Wehrmacht overran a continent.

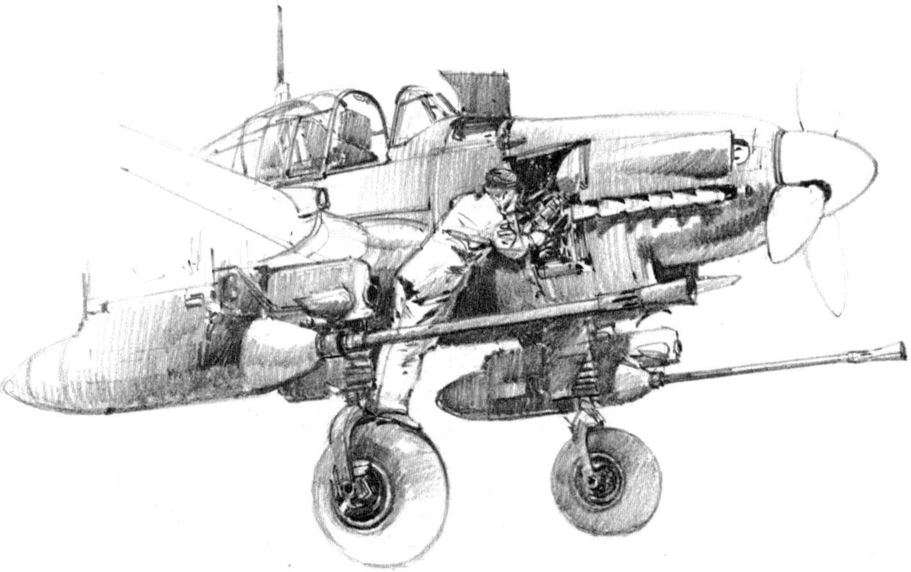

The Ambulance that wasn't always – Heinkel He 59

Originally designed in 1930 as a reconnaissance bomber capable of being flown with either wheel or float undercarriage, the twin-engine Heinkel He 59 biplane survived only as a seaplane, being first flown as such in January 1932. Powered by two 660-hp BMW liquid-cooled engines and armed with single defensive machine guns in nose, dorsal and ventral positions, the He 59B-2 floatplane first saw action during the Spanish Civil War when a small number was used by the Condor Legion for night bombing and anti-shipping patrols.

By the outbreak of War in September 1939 the He 59C–without bomb aimer's position in the nose–had been introduced, the bomber version having been withdrawn from service. Henceforth the old biplane would be employed largely for maritime reconnaissance and air-sea rescue. For these duties it equipped the *Seenotdienststaffeln* (air-sea rescue squadrons) based on the coasts of the North Sea and Baltic, as well as the third *Staffeln* of the coastal reconnaissance groups (*Küstenfliegergruppen*), namely *3./Ku.Fl.Gr. 106, 406, 506* and *706*. Approximately 80 He 59s were included in the Luftwaffe's Order of Battle at the time of the Polish campaign.

However one other He 59 unit deserves special mention, for the Luftwaffe had foreseen the need to set aside a number of the seaplanes for special duties. *Staffel Schwilben* had been formed in 1939 for the purpose of transporting relatively small groups of troops to carry out amphibious attacks against hostile shores. Two such minor operations were carried out on the Baltic Coast during the Polish campaign, but it was during the invasion of Norway that *Staffel Schwilben* was heavily engaged. In the last three weeks of April 1940 the dozen or so seaplanes were flown into numerous fjords on the rugged coastline to deliver parties of up to 50 soldiers who paddled ashore in rubber boats to attack some key point or block a road along which Norwegian forces had to travel. Later, as the German army fought its way northwards, the He 59s were used to deliver stores, mail and medical supplies as well as to evacuate seriously wounded personnel. For the latter work *Staffel Schwilben* borrowed specially-equipped He 59C-2 ambulances from the *Seenotdienst*.

The He 59's most spectacular operation was however to be carried out on the first day of Hitler's attack in the West, May 10, 1940. One of the key objectives to ensure a swift and successful invasion of the Low Countries was to be the seizure of the twin

8Y

bridges over the Maas at Rotterdam. At seven o'clock that morning six He 59s approached the bridge from the west as six more flew in from the east, alighted on the Nieuwe Maas and disgorged 120 assault troops who swiftly paddled for the shore and set up their heavy machine guns on the Willems Bridge, soon to be joined by 50 paratroops, dropped nearby by Junkers Ju 52/3ms. As four of the Heinkel seaplanes succumbed to Dutch gunfire, the eight survivors took off to return to their base on the Zwischenahner Meer, 150 miles to the north-east. For this operation *Staffel Schwilben* had been temporarily redesignated *Kampfgruppe zur Besonderen Verwendung 108* (Battle Group on Special Operations 108).

By the time the Battle of Britain opened in July that year the *Seenotdienst* had set up bases in a number of the Channel ports, notably Ostend, Calais, Boulogne, Le Havre, Cherbourg, St Malo and Brest. The task of the seaplanes was to be vital to the Luftwaffe. It quickly

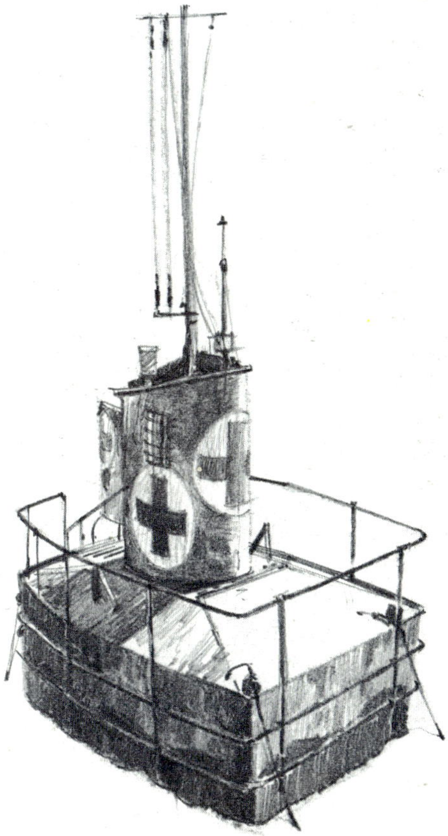

Above: *a floating refuge for ditched aircrew*

Left: *ideal for work in Norway, the Heinkel He 59 was able to use the confined waters of the fjords to provide communications with German garrison forces based on the long coastline*

became evident that a high proportion of the battles being fought against the RAF would be well out over the sea, and quite large numbers of airmen would require rescue. Another problem soon arose as the pilots of relatively short range fighters, heavily committed to combat over England, found themselves desperately short of fuel for their return flight and were often forced to ditch.

The RAF seldom recognised the Luftwaffe's right to recover its airmen from the sea to fight another day, the immunity of the He 59 being finally ended by Churchill himself following evidence that at least some of the 'ambulance' aircraft were shadowing British convoys and radioing their positions. Moreover at least two such seaplanes (of *Staffel Schwilben*) were shot down while sowing mines in the Thames Estuary. The differentiation between *bona fide* rescue aircraft and those engaged in more sinister activities was often too academic in the blur of combat. And it must be remarked that in the score of He 59s shot down in the Battle of Britain there was scarcely a crew member qualified to render first aid, while the casualty lists included a remarkably high proportion of senior Luftwaffe and Kriegsmarine officers–surely unusual crew members for aircraft engaged solely in rescue work. . .

Flying Pencil – Dornier Do 17

Forever remembered as the 'Flying Pencil' on account of its original slim lines, the Dornier Do 17 was very nearly discarded before it even entered service, yet was to become a cornerstone of the Luftwaffe's bomber force during the first year of the Second World War.

Originally conceived as a high-speed passenger mailplane for Lufthansa, three Do 17 prototypes were produced in 1934 but were discarded out of hand by the airline as it was thought that no passenger would ever fly in the aircraft a second time owing to the excessively cramped and uncomfortable cabin compartments! The otherwise beautiful shoulder-wing monoplane possessed two such cabins measuring roughly 5 ft in diameter and 7 ft long in each of which three passengers were expected to sit. Despite a speed of almost 250 mph the aircraft were returned to Löwenthal where they were put into storage.

When however an RLM pilot, Flugkapitän Robert Untucht, heard of the unwanted aircraft he gained permission to fly one and was so impressed by its performance that he suggested to the Ministry's Technical Department that it might be reconsidered as a bomber. Untucht was by no means without influence with Ernst Udet, having gained an armful of international speed records for Germany in the Heinkel He 70 in 1933. A man after Udet's own heart, he was to be killed when one of the Ju 90 prototypes crashed during tropical trials at Bathurst in November 1938.

Capable of carrying a modest 1,100-lb bomb load – roughly comparable with the early British Bristol Blenheim – the Do 17E entered production in 1936, together with the 17F reconnaissance version. A small number of each was sent to Spain where they gave good service and proved faster than any of the opposing fighters available in 1937; later experience was to show that mere level speed was not enough to escape interceptors which dived from above, and recommendations were soon being made to improve the Do 17's defensive armament, hitherto a single machine gun.

The next major production versions, which appeared at the beginning of 1938 were the Do 17M bomber and the 17P reconnaissance aircraft, the former powered by 900-hp Bramo radials and the latter by 865 hp BMW radials. With the lessons learned in Spain the bomber was now armed with three guns and could carry twice the bomb load of the E version. Despite the increased power the bomber's performance suffered badly, and opinions within the Luftwaffe remained deeply divided on the relative merits of defensive armament and performance.

Kampfgeschwader 2, *whose aircraft are seen here over the Arc de Triomphe in Paris during 1940, was probably the most famous of all Dornier Do 17 Wings, but suffered heavily in the Battle of Britain*

Unfortunately the Dornier suffered the worst sort of compromise and, because of the large scale production undertaken in 1938-39, the shortcomings demonstrated early in the War were to influence bomber design throughout a critical period in the Luftwaffe's fortunes.

Although many of the older versions remained in service, the outbreak of War found the new Dornier Do 17Z already established as the most-used bomber on the *Kampfgeschwader*. This version, with an entirely redesigned, deeper and extensively glazed nose and powered by 1,000-hp Bramo engines, was armed with four guns. During the Polish campaign it equipped *KG 2* *<Holzhammer>* ('Wooden Hammer'), *KG 3* *<Blitz>* ('Lightning'), *KG 76* and *KG 77*. The two first-named Wings were deployed on the Northern Front, *KG 2* carrying out a number of very long distance raids, including one to Biala-Podlaska on the eastern border with Russia near Brest Litovsk; *KG 3* was largely engaged in attacks along Poland's Baltic coast. *KG 77* flew mainly against industrial targets in the south, including Crakow and Krosno, while *KG 76* was employed to strike rail centres at Kielce, Lodz, Radom, Skierniewice and Tomaszów in front of Warsaw and in the south. It was however *KG 77* that participated in the devastating raid on the Polish capital on September 25.

In the euphoria that pervaded the German forces at the conclusion of the short Polish campaign (despite the relatively heavy loss of some 200 aircraft and about 430 aircrew killed) some serious shortcomings in the German aircraft–although reported to the RLM–were either brushed aside with little investigation or simply ignored altogether. In particular the very poor disposition of the defensive armament of the Do 17, and the lack of adequate field of fire for its gunners, went unremedied–with serious results for the *Kampfgeschwader* less than a year hence. It is most likely that, with increasing deliveries of the Heinkel He 111 and Junkers Ju 88 bombers–and a confidence in the Wehrmacht's ability to finish the War quickly–the RLM saw no urgency in extensive modification to an aircraft that would probably disappear from service altogether sometime in 1940.

Dorniers over England – Do 17

There can be little doubt that Hitler's conduct of the War in 1940 caught the Luftwaffe somewhat ill-prepared to perform operational tasks that fell beyond the scope of direct support of the Wehrmacht. Certainly when flown over the 'conventional' land battle, as in Poland, the Low Countries and France, it proved invincible. However it has been argued with likely justification that, in the absence of a true strategic bombing force, any invasion of Britain might well have failed altogether.

At the beginning of the Battle of Britain the Luftwaffe fielded three types of medium bomber, the Heinkel He 111, the Dornier Do 17 and the Junkers Ju 88, in that order of numerical strength. All were capable of reaching the main centres of population and industry in Britain from their bases in France and

Scandinavia–with somewhat reduced bomb load–but all were extremely vulnerable to fighter interception when flown in daylight, not least the Do 17. In July 1940 there were still nine Gruppen with Do 17Zs, namely *I*, *II* and *III./KG 2* <*Holzhammer*>, *I*, *II* and *III./KG 3*<*Blitz*>, *I* and *III./KG 76* and *Küstenfliegergruppe 606* (the latter largely crewed by the Kriegsmarine but later redesignated *Kampfgruppe 606*). All were based in France and the Low Countries as components of *Luftflotte 2* under the command of Albert Kesselring.

The air attacks of July were relatively short range raids aimed at British convoys in the Channel. The first major attack was launched by 26 Do 17Zs of *I./KG 2* on the 10th against a convoy in the Straits of Dover; despite heavy protection by Messerschmitts, two Hurricane squadrons (including No 111 whose pilots engaged in head-on attacks– particularly effective against the Do 17) managed to get through to the bombers and shoot down three, including the aircraft of a *Staffelkapitan*. Another of the *Geschwader's Staffelkapitäne* was to be lost two days later off the Suffolk coast.

This early setback for *KG 2* led to the provision of heavier escorts by Bf 109 fighters–an expedient that proved distinctly unpopular among the *Jagdverbande*–but which certainly limited bomber losses for a short time. When however Göring's main air attacks opened early in August the calls for fighter protection were coming in from all the bomber units, so that individual formations were necessarily less well protected. *KG 2's* losses continued to mount slowly until, on August 13, 74 of the *Geschwader's* Dorniers set out to attack the airfield at Eastchurch. Led by the *Geschwaderkommodore* himself, Oberst Johannes Fink (who had been awarded the Knight's Cross during the Battle of France), the Dornier crews, unaware that the raid had been recalled and therefore deprived of their fighter escort, were caught by two Hurricane squadrons and one of Spitfires which shot down five of the raiders and damaged five others. On the 18th it was *KG 76's* turn when, led by Oberstleutnant Stefan Frölich over Kent and the Thames Estuary, it was met by three Hurricane and two Spitfire squadrons: six Dorniers and two Ju 88s, whose crews included two more *Staffelkapitäne*, were lost.

By the end of the great daylight raids of Sunday September 15–often regarded as the climax of the Battle–total combat casualties among the Do 17 Geschwader amounted to 136 aircraft destroyed and almost as many damaged (of which Fink's *KG 2* lost 51, as well as a *Gruppenkommandeur* and seven *Staffelkapitäne*). From the earliest days of the great Battle some of the more experienced RAF pilots had been able to work out the best way to attack the Dornier which proved to be extremely vulnerable to beam attacks from slightly below as well as the head-on attacks which were almost exclusive to the Hurricane pilots of Nos 32 and 111 Squadrons.

Yet for all its high casualty rate the Dornier gained something of a reputation for its ability to withstand battle damage, there being numerous instances of aircraft returning on one engine or with controls shot away. In one famous raid on Biggin Hill airfield on August 18 an attack by nine *KG 76* Dorniers was met by Spitfires which shot down two of the raiders; in one of the surviving aircraft the pilot was killed but the flight engineer, Feldwebel Wilhelm-Friedrich Illg, took control and brought the bomber home to a safe landing in France; awarded the Knight's Cross for his action, Illg was to be shot down a week later and taken prisoner.

Not surprisingly it was with some relief that the Do 17's withdrawal from service was speeded up during the autumn of 1940 (although it was to be reinstated as

a makeshift night fighter), and the six remaining Gruppen employed almost exclusively in the night bombing rôle during the winter Blitz of 1940-41. In the anonymity of night operations the Do 17 suffered no better nor worse than the other German bombers.

Harsh Russian Front winter conditions forced the Luftwaffe to adopt all manner of expedients to keep flying. The yellow 'theatre' band on this Do 17 denotes service in the East

The Graceful Whale – Dornier Do 18

One of the most attractive flying boats ever produced must surely have been the Dornier Do 18 which equipped Germany's coastal reconnaissance units during the first two years of the War. It also gained a place in the pages of history as the first hostile aeroplane to fall to the guns of British aircraft in the Second World War.

Origins of the Do 18 can be traced as far back as November 6, 1922 when the first Dornier *Wal* (Whale) made its first flight. Forbidden to build flying boats under the post-War restrictions, Dornier established a company in Italy (CMASA) to build *Wal*; in due course they were also produced in Spain, Holland and Japan before production switched to Germany in 1932 where Dornier's factory at Friedrichshafen on the shores of Lake Constance began building the aircraft for Luthansa (with this airline they made no fewer than 328 mail-carrying crossings of the South Atlantic) and, soon after, for the new Luftwaffe which designated them Do 15. In 1934 Lufthansa ordered a development of the *Wal*, the Do 18 which first flew on March 15, 1935; in March 1938 one of the commercial aircraft established a world distance record of 5,214 miles, flying to Brazil after being catapulted from its depot ship *Westfalen* in the English Channel.

A high-wing monoplane with stub sponsons to provide stability on the water, the Do 18 was powered by a pair of engines (initially Jumo 205s) mounted in tandem on the wing above the pylon and clear of spray while taxying, taking off and landing. Although the Do 18 was primarily developed for Lufthansa North and South Atlantic services–where it established a fine record of reliability–the Luftwaffe expressed interest in the aircraft in 1936 as a replacement for the earlier Do 15s, and production of the military Do 18D the following year. This version, with 600-hp Jumo 205C engines, a crew of four and an armament of two light machine guns in open bow and midships positions, entered service in September 1939 for coastal reconnaissance over the North Sea and Baltic.

The Do 18Ds were joined and eventually replaced by a more powerful version, the Do 18G with 880-hp Jumo 205D engines, in 1939, this aircraft mounting a 20-mm cannon in a midships power-operated turret and a heavy machine gun (13-mm) in the bow position. These aircraft were delivered to the

MICHAEL TURNER

Küstenfliegergruppen, with which they usually equipped the second Staffel.

Production of the Do 18 was in fact terminated at the outbreak of War, by which time about 30 Ds and 70 Gs had been produced. These boats, based at ports in Northern Germany, commenced patrols from September 1 over the North Sea, keeping watch for ships of the Royal Navy which might venture out from Scapa Flow to interfere with the sea trials of Germany's new battleships, the *Scharnhorst* and *Gneisenau*. Indeed the capital ships of Admiral Forbes' Home Fleet started patrolling between Iceland and Norway to intercept German merchant shipping on September 3. It was on the 26th of that month that crews of three Do 18s of *2./Ku.Fl.Gr.506* spotted the British fleet, comprising the battleships HMS *Nelson*, *Rodney* and *Repulse*, the battlecruisers HMS *Hood* and *Renown*, the carrier HMS *Ark Royal*, two cruisers and ten destroyers, and began to shadow them, reporting back the fleet's position and course. As a force of Ju 88s set out from German bases HMS *Ark Royal* launched nine Skuas, whose pilots attacked and shot down one of the Dorniers and drove off the other two. The four crew members of the downed aircraft (credited to Lieut S. B. McEwen RN of No 803 Squadron) were rescued by HMS *Somali* whose gunners then destroyed

Following successful commercial use of seaplane tenders the Dornier Do 18 (a Do 18D-1 of Kü.Fl.Gr 306 *is shown here) saw limited service with such ships during the War to extend its patrol range*

the Do 18. The fleet was eventually attacked by the Ju 88s, near misses but no hits being scored (giving rise to the first of several German claims to have sunk the *Ark Royal*).

By the time of the Battle of Britain the number of units operational on the Do 18 had fallen to four, namely *2.Staffel*, *Kü.Fl.Gr.106* with six boats distributed between St Malo, Brest and Lorient, and the three *Staffeln* of *Kü.Fl.Gr.406* whose 37 boats were based at seaplane stations as widely separated as Stavanger in Norway and Calais in France. While ostensibly the duty of their crews was still to keep watch for British naval vessels, their responsibilities also embraced air-sea rescue, calibration of both shipborne and shore radar, watch for possible escapees from German-occupied territories and liaison with German U-boats in coastal waters. A total of 12 Do 18s was lost from all causes during the period of the Battle of Britain, and a glance at some of theses causes provide clues to the multifarious nature of the jobs undertaken: five shot down while in the vicinity of British convoys, two lost in a night take-off collision at Stavanger, one (of *2./106*) lost while taking off with personnel picked up from the south coast of Ireland, and one sunk while under tow off the far north coast of Norway less than 30 miles from the Russian border.

In 1942 some of the surviving boats were modified (as the Do 18N) for exclusive air-sea rescue duties and, with armament removed, joined the *Seenotdienst* for service in the Baltic, Black Sea and Mediterranean. Despite carrying prominent Red Cross markings the suspicion lurked among Germany's enemies that their duties were not what they appeared to be and, when spotted, were seldom given the benefit of doubt.

Heyday of the Heinkel – He 111

The Heinkel He 111 was unusual among the Luftwaffe's early wartime bombers in that its crew positions were not concentrated in the extreme nose, as in the Do 17 and Ju 88. Being a larger and much heavier aircraft, it accommodated a five-man crew, compared to four crew members in the other aircraft. It was also better defended, possessing up to six machine guns in nose, ventral, beam and dorsal positions.

At the beginning of the War the standard He 111P with 1,150-hp DB 601 engines was being joined by the He 111H with Jumo engines, the latter version remaining in production until early 1944. Both the H and P series differed considerably from the earlier models in adopting near-straight tapered wings and smooth-contoured, fully-glazed nose (with its curious offset spherical gun position). These early aircraft were able to lift up to 4,000 lb of bombs (frequently a pair of 2,200-lb weapons).

In the shortlived but bitter campaign against Poland the raids launched by *KG 1* <*Hindenburg*>, *KG 4* <*General Wever*>, *KG 26* <*Löwen*> ('Lion'), *KG 53* <*Legion Cóndor*>, *I/KG 152* and *II./LG 2*, were truly devastating. On that first day some 330 He 111s were sent against Polish cities and airfields where enormous damage was wrought. For example *II./KG 4*, led by Oberst Walter Erdmann, dropped 22 tons of bombs on the airfield at Lemburg, while *II./LG 1* bombed Warsaw-Okecie airfield where the vital PZL aircraft factory was hit. Warsaw itself was the target of 90 Heinkels of *KG 27*. During the latter half of the campaign *KG 4*, under Oberst Martin Fiebig, took over the task of reducing the capital in an obvious attempt to persuade the civilian population to leave the city, whose ultimate capture would otherwise be accompanied by heavy loss of life, five leaflet raids were carried out prior to the final assault. The great raid on Warsaw of September 25 by upwards of 260 German bombers was intended to overcome the Poles' final resistance–it came to epitomise the ruthless nature of German bombing–it was said that more than 2,600 perished, of whom almost half were civilians. Long before then the Polish air force had ceased to exist . . .

In the Norwegian campaign the Heinkels' long range and performance was put to good effect, three Gruppen being deployed, of which *KG 26* <*Löwen*> was particularly effective in its attacks on ships of the Royal Navy. However when *III./KG 26* started to operate from a frozen lake a sudden thaw caused one of the Heinkels to sink through the ice; only the prompt order by Major Viktor von Lossberg (later to be awarded the Knight's Cross in 1941 as a pathfinder leader) for the other aircraft to jettison their bombs and take off saved his *Gruppe* from total loss.

Meanwhile the first bombs had fallen on British soil, and a Heinkel He 111H of *KG 26's* Staff Flight had been the first to fall to the RAF's guns over land when Leutnant Rolf Niehoff's aircraft was shot down near the Firth of Forth on October 28, 1939.

Heinkel He 111s of the 'Lion Wing', Kampfgeschwader 26, *over London during the Winter Blitz. Despite blackout precautions navigation to the British capital seldom presented problems for the German crews*

It was the Luftwaffe's He 111s that were to be involved in one of the War's great bombing tragedies. On May 14 during the German invasion of Holland, Rotterdam, which had withstood all attacks by the Wehrmacht for four days, began negotiating with the local German commander for the surrender of the city. At that moment about one hundred aircraft of *KG 54*, led by Oberst Lackner, were already on their way under orders to attack, but by the time a radio message had been sent out recalling the raiders their bomb aimers (who doubled as radio operators) had switched off their sets to set up their bomb sights. The first wave of 30 bombers had already dropped its bombs when fortunately the leader of the second spotted a signal flare fired from the ground indicating cancellation of the raid. However the concentration of bombs already dropped – some 97 tons – killed more than 800 civilians in the centre of the city.

The heavy casualties suffered by the Heinkel He 111 in the Battle of Britain reflected the greater use of the aircraft rather than any particular vulnerability to fighter attack; indeed RAF pilots tended to regard the He 111 as a 'rather hard nut to crack'. No fewer than 18 Gruppen of these bombers (totalling about 600 aircraft at any one time) were launched against Britain, flying some of the heaviest and most destructive raids of the Battle. The total loss of some 280 aircraft in combat during the daylight attacks was probably of less importance to the Luftwaffe than that of the large number of crew members; the loss of commanders, especially on the He 111 units, included the *Geschwaderkommodoren*, Oberst Georgi of *KG 27* and Oberst Stöckl of *KG 55*, no fewer than seven *Gruppenkommandeuren* and 12 *Staffelkapitäne*. The German aircraft industry might soon replace the aircraft–and did–but their experienced crews and commanders could never be replaced.

A Heinkel He 111H causes a minor snowstorm as it taxies in the Russian winter; effective camouflage was difficult, the Luftwaffe roughly daubing its aircraft with white distemper

Bombers no Longer Needed – Heinkel He 111

The change to night bombing which came about gradually from mid-September 1940 onwards, and which came to be known as the Blitz, must have been something of a relief to the battle-shocked crews of Göring's bombers, despite their general lack of training in night operations. Already German scientists had evolved a simple system of radio beams (code-named *Knickbein*, or 'crooked leg') which, picked up by specially-equipped Heinkel He 111s, enabled their crews to navigate to their target. This system was soon rendered useless by British jamming but a new, more complex equipment known as *X-Gerät* ('X-gear') came into use in the late summer of 1940 which enabled the special He 111 pathfinder unit, *Kampfgruppe 100* led by Hauptmann Friedrich Aschenbrenner, to indicate to a bomber stream the whereabouts of a particular target. Probably the most famous raid involving the pathfinder Heinkels of *KGr 100* was that carried out by 449 He 111s, Do 17s and Ju 88s on the Midlands industrial city of Coventry on November 14, 1940 which killed 400 and injured twice that number.

Many British provincial towns and cities felt the weight of German bombs during that long winter, and London suffered more than 50 raids on consecutive nights. Being by far the greatest weightlifter, the He 111 dropped the heaviest tonnage of bombs which included the hated 'parachute mine'. In reality this was an adaptation of the naval magnetic mine fitted with a barometric fuse; set to detonate several feet above the ground these weapons caused considerable flattening of buildings by virtue of the blast effect.

At first British night fighters were almost non-existent, but gradually new airborne intercept (AI) radar came into service and was mastered by the crews of the newly-introduced Beaufighter which, early in 1941, began to take a mounting toll of the night raiders.

By May however Hitler's attention had turned eastwards towards Russia and, in preparation for the great attack, the Heinkels of *KG 4*, *KG 27*, *KG 53* and *KG 55* were withdrawn from the West and moved to bases in Poland. Never again was the Luftwaffe able to assemble on a single front so many bombers as it had against England. Indeed the Heinkels were now to be scattered throughout Europe and elsewhere. *III./KG 40* remained in France, now tasked with anti-shipping duties, as were *I.* and *III./KG 26* in Norway. *II./KG 26* was split between Sicily and Libya, while part of *KG 4* was deployed in Romania whence its Heinkels started sowing mines in the Suez Canal; some were sent to Iraq to bolster the pro-Axis revolution under Raschid Ali.

The diversity of duties now thrust upon the He 111 is evidence of the Luftwaffe's disenchantment with use of its bombers in a strategic rôle: targets abounded in the West and in the East yet there were no means to reach and destroy them. Instead the Heinkels of the Norway-based *KG 26* were adapted to carry torpedoes for use against the North Cape convoys, their first successful action being against convoy PQ 17 in July 1942 when *I./KG* 26 sank five ships for the loss of two aircraft. Two months later the Geschwader torpedoed eight vessels but retribution was swift when Sea Hurricanes from the carrier HMS *Avenger* shot down six of the He 111s and severely damaged nine others.

On the Eastern Front the Wehrmacht's fortunes fluctuated after its initial smashing advance to the gates of Moscow and deep into the Caucasus. When its Sixth Army was trapped in the ruins of Stalingrad orders went out to assemble every available He 111 that had been converted for transport use (including many of the old D and F versions) to supply the beleaguered troops. At the height of the airlift some 290 Heinkels were flying stores into the pocket, occasionally reverting to their bombing rôle as Soviet tanks threatened their landing strips. When eventually resistance by the doomed army ended in February 1943 the Luftwaffe had lost 165 of its Heinkels, many of which had been borrowed from front line bomber units. It was a loss from which the *Kampfgeschwader* were never to recover.

Eighteen months later Heinkels returned once more to an assault on Britain, in a manner unique at the time. Following the capture of the flying bomb sites in France, *III./KG 3* was re-formed to fly He 111H-22s adapted to *carry* a V1 under the wing root. By the time its bases at Gilze Rijen and Venlo had been captured by the Allies the Gruppe had discharged 300 bombs against London, 90 against Southampton and 20 against Gloucester. Moving back to bases in Germany the Gruppe was joined by two others which, with about 100 He 111s, launched a further 800 bombs against Britain. However RAF Mosquitos shot down some 70 of the Heinkels before these operations ended on January 14, 1945.

Perhaps the strangest of all He 111s was the He 111Z (Z for *Zwilling*, or Twin) which, for towing the huge Messerschmitt Me 321 *Gigant* gliders, comprised two standard He 111Hs joined together. These extraordinary aircraft saw service, particularly behind the Eastern Front where much of the movement of supplies was undertaken by gliders.

Emil – Messerschmitt Bf 109E

Produced in larger numbers than any other German aircraft, Willi Messerschmitt's immortal 'one-oh-nine' stands alongside the British Spitfire and the American P-51 Mustang among the greatest fighters of all time; moreover its pilots destroyed by far the largest number of hostile aircraft of any in history.

An almost exact contemporary of Sydney Camm's Hawker Hurricane, the first prototype made its maiden flight at Augsburg in September 1935, flown by Flugkapitän 'Bubi' Knötsch. It had been designed to compete with three other aircraft, the Arado Ar 80, Focke-Wulf Fw 159 and Heinkel He 112, for a monoplane fighter to replace the He 51 and Ar 68 biplanes. When flown in the Travemünde competition, from which it emerged the winner, the 109 prototype was powered by a British Rolls-Royce Kestrel, but later aircraft featured the Jumo 210.

The production Bf 109B appeared in 1937 and 40 such aircraft were sent for service with the Condor Legion in Spain where, flown by such foremost pilots as Werner Mölders, Wolfgang Schellmann and Reinhard Seiler, these and the later 109Cs and Es ruled the skies. As a *Staffelführer* in Spain, Mölders evolved the fighting tactics based on the formation of four aircraft–the *Schwarm*–which later became adopted throughout the world for air combat.

The first major production version, which entered Luftwaffe service in 1938, was the Bf 109E, widely known among its pilots as the Emil. Possibly the best-liked of all the 109s, the Emil possessed that indefinable 'feel' of an aeroplane whose combination of power, wing loading and control sensitivity seems to inspire confidence as well as bestowing something of an individual character. Such character is often in evidence only early in an aeroplane's life when one becomes aware of what the designer has been trying to achieve, before the military theorists start adding more and bigger guns, increasing the engine power and hanging things on it until it becomes a leaden object in one's hands.

When the War started the Bf 109E was superior to any other fighter in the world–even the Spitfire–although some of its pilots were already questioning its relatively light armament of two machine guns and either one or two cannon; on some versions the single 20-mm cannon was located between the engine's cylinder banks to fire through the propeller hub, thereby obviating the need for synchronising gear.

The Polish campaign proved to be a combat walkover for the Emil and it was indeed a brave man who pitted the obsolete PZL fighter against the fast, nimble 109. Nevertheless a number of Luftwaffe pilots were killed early in the War, often as the result of accidents after combat, for the little fighter's narrow undercarriage demanded special care when landing–particularly on rough grass airfields; this characteristic was to go unremedied throughout the 109's life.

Apart from an occasional fleeting brush with German fighters over the Maginot Line in France, the RAF's first real taste of action against the Emil occurred on December 18, 1939 when 22 unescorted Wellingtons tried to fly an armed reconnaissance in daylight over the Heligoland Bight. Warned by radar the Luftwaffe ordered off 34 Bf 109Es and 16 Bf 110s to intercept. Only ten Wellingtons landed back at base. . .

Large numbers of Bf 109Es were flown in the Battle of France where they quickly proved superior to the French Dewoitine D.520 and Hawker Hurricane. By the end of that campaign Hauptmann Wilhelm Balthasar (*Staffelkapitän* of 7./*JG* 27 and a veteran of Spain) had emerged as top scorer of the Luftwaffe in France with 22 victories. However the first real test for the Emil was now at hand.

The Bf 109 had been designed as an interceptor and a fighter intended to maintain air cover over a ground battle, so that the combats which constituted the Battle of Britain imposed considerable strains upon the Emil pilots. Even when permitted to engage in *frei Jagd* (free chase) missions over Southern England, the approaching German fighters were frequently spotted on British radar so that RAF fighters could be scrambled to meet them; then after combat, short of fuel, the German pilots were faced with a long haul back across the Channel to their bases. Furthermore the relative failure of the bigger Bf 110 as an effective escort fighter resulted in the Emil pilots being ordered to take on escort duties for the lumbering bomber formations, the very antithesis of the 109's true function.

Widely regarded as one of the greatest of all fighter pilots, Werner Mölders is seen here destroying a French Curtiss Hawk over BEF troops during their retreat to Dunkirk in 1940

When wiser counsels prevailed towards the end of August and the *Jagdgeschwader* were once more given free rein, the 109 truly came into its own: in the space of a fortnight the Emil pilots alone destroyed a total of 120 Hurricanes, 93 Spitfires and 12 Defiants–for the loss of 167 of their own number. Had not Göring committed the cardinal sin of shifting his aim from the destruction of the British fighter defences and started bombing London on September 7, the Emil had it in its power to destroy RAF Fighter Command on its own! After all, every one of the *Jagdgeschwader* remained intact–something that could not be said for the British fighter squadrons . . .

Fighters for Barbarossa – Messerschmitt Bf 109F

The Battle of Britain ended in the autumn of 1940 with the Luftwaffe frustrated in its object of winning air superiority over Britain by day and with RAF Fighter Command tattered but intact. Arguments now gained currency among German fighter pilots who began to criticise the 109's lack of hitting power. The true experts (and by the end of the Battle of Britain there were several who had passed the 40-victory mark) tended to favour fewer but bigger guns, their superior marksmanship resulting in economic use of effective ammunition, while lesser pilots preferred to fire longer bursts with a better chance of obtaining some hits. In this respect the Emil's two cannon (when fitted) had probably been no less effective than the eight guns of the Spitfire and Hurricane with their rifle calibre. Mölders went further however and suggested personally to Göring that more engine power was needed if the 109 was to retain its superiority.

Such a version, the Bf 109F, first appeared in service in May 1941, by which time the improved Spitfire V was displaying a distinct superiority over the old Emil. Powered by a 1,300-hp DB 601 in a new symmetrical cowling, the 109F retained the single cannon and twin machine gun armament, much to the disgust of

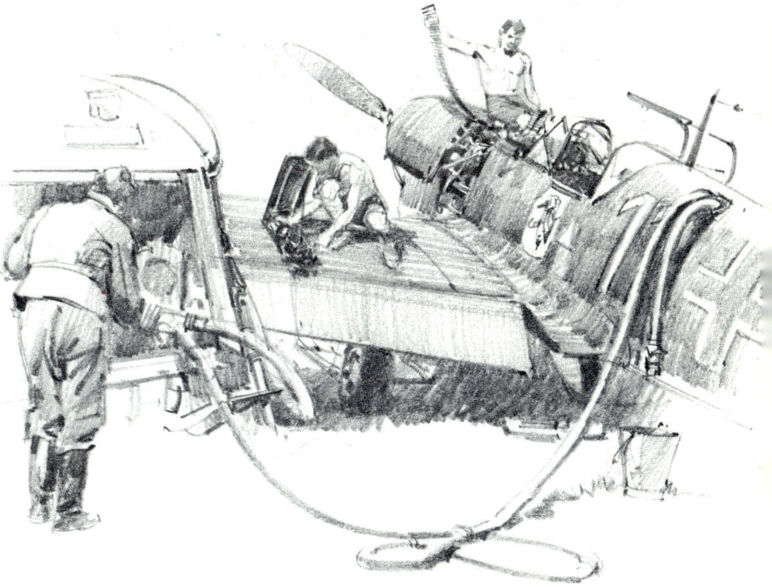

Galland who argued on behalf of the average pilot rather than himself (he had after all reached the 60-kill mark). Even Walter Oesau (a veteran of Spain and by now holder of a score of more than 40 victories) preferred to fly his old Emil with two cannon and two machine guns until a lack of spares forced him to adopt the new aircraft.

By now Galland was *Geschwaderkommodore* of *JG 26* <*Schlageter*>, while his great friend and rival Mölders led *JG 51*, both based in France. However the spring of 1941 found Göring redeploying his forces in readiness for the great attack on Russia, and Mölders was ordered to move his Geschwader's Bf 109Fs to the East. By this time his personal score had reached 68 victories. Galland and his *JG 26*, as well as *JG 2* <*Richthofen*> under Oesau, were left behind as the only fighters in France, as Major Günther Lutzow's *JG 3* <*Udet*> (Bf 109Fs), *II.* and *III./JG 27* (Bf 109Es) under Schellmann, *II.* and *III./JG 52* (Bf 109Es) under Major Hans Trübenbach, *JG 53* (Bf 109Fs) under Major Günther von Maltzahn, *JG 54* <*Grünherz*> ('Green Hearts', Bf 109s) under Major Hannes Trautloft and *JG 77* (Bf 109Es) under Major Bernhard Woldenga all moved to the East. It is perhaps worth remarking that the eight fighter leaders just mentioned were ultimately to amass personal victory totals which combined added up to 601; all but Trübenbach were to be awarded Knight's Crosses.

The Bf 109F's great moment arrived on June 22, 1941 when Germany's armies smashed their way forward over the length of the vast Eastern Front. Often carrying loads of small fragmentation bombs the Luftwaffe's fighters roamed far and wide, strafing every Soviet airfield within 60 miles of the front, shooting up and bombing the enemy aircraft caught unprepared on the ground. Occasionally Russian fighters managed to take off but most were instantly overwhelmed. During the first 24 hours German pilots claimed to have destroyed more than 1,800 Russian aircraft – the Soviets admitted losing 1,200. Eight days later Mölders' Wing claimed its 1,000th enemy destroyed; by August 15 all the 109 Wings had reached or passed that score.

Meanwhile an Emil *Gruppe*, *I./JG 27* led by Hauptmann Eduard Neumann, had been deployed to North Africa to support Erwin Rommel's Afrika Korps. By the end of the year it had been joined by the Geschwader's two other Gruppen and was re-equipping with Bf 109Fs which quickly established their superiority over all opposing RAF fighters. It was on *3.Staffel* that a 22-year-old Leutnant began to emerge as a truly outstanding exponent of the 109.

Hans-Joachim Marseille had previously fought over the English Channel in 1940 where he had destroyed seven Spitfires but, in the process had himself been shot down four times. On arrival in Africa he found the desert skies seemed to suit his keen eyesight and uncanny 'three dimensional vision'. On September 24, 1941 he shot down five Allied aircraft in a single day, but as soon as he got his hands on a 109F his rate of scoring quickened. On February 22, 1942 he was awarded the Knight's Cross when his tally reached 50. On June 3 he downed six aircraft in eleven minutes, but bettered this on September 1 when he shot down 17 RAF fighters in three sorties – 16 Kittyhawks and a Spitfire. For this extraordinary achievement Marseille was awarded the Diamonds (his Oakleaves *and* Swords having both been awarded in June).

JG 27's *Messerschmitt Bf 109Fs provide top cover for Stukas as they take off from a Western Desert airstrip early in 1942. This Geschwader bore the brunt of air combat in North Africa*

As if to emphasise the superiority of the 109F in the West, Galland was given charge of organising the fighter cover during the escape of the German warships *Scharnhorst*, *Gneisenau* and *Prinz Eugen* up the Channel in February 1942. The Luftwaffe put up some 200 fighters–the great majority of them Bf 109Fs–and when eventually the RAF made hasty efforts to attack the German naval squadron these fighters shot down 49 British aircraft, albeit it must be admitted including such antiquated machines as the Swordfish biplanes led by Lieut-Cdr Eugene Esmonde RN, for the loss of only four of their own number.

The Gustav – Messerschmitt Bf 109G

Even as the F-model was imposing its influence on the air war in all the main war theatres early in 1942 a new version was about to start delivery to the *Jagdgeschwader*. The Bf 109G–universally known as the Gustav–featured the 1,475-hp DB 605 engine with increased compression, but apart from 13-mm machine guns replacing the earlier rifle-calibre weapons on the nose, was scarcely distinguishable from the F version. The larger nose guns however necessitated prominent fairings over the breeches giving rise to the Gustav's other nickname, the *Beule* (Boil or Bump).

The annals of the Gustav opened tragically in Africa when the engine of Marseille's aircraft failed over the desert on September 30, 1942; he attempted to bale out but was struck by the tailplane and killed. The death of Marseille, whose ultimate victory tally of 158 was the highest of any pilot in the West, had a

profoundly demoralising effect on his fellow pilots, coming as it did as Axis fortunes approached their nadir in North Africa. Already Ernst Udet had died by his own hand, depressed and disillusioned, and the great Mölders had been killed in a flying accident on his way to the funeral.

Furthermore, as the Wehrmacht reeled under the enormous defeat at Stalingrad, the winter of 1942–43 found the German homeland feeling the first weight of American bombs in daylight. Hitherto only one single-seat interceptor fighter *Gruppe*, *I./JG 1* with Gustavs, had been tasked with the daylight defence of Germany, but early in 1943 a new *Geschwader*, *JG 11* under Major Anton Mader, came into being, this unit being generally regarded as the pioneer among the huge fighter forces that were soon to fight the formations of American B-17s and B-24s which were to fly deeper and deeper into Europe during the next two years. Henceforth the story of the Messerschmitt Bf 109 was to be increasingly concerned with what became known as The Defence of the Reich.

From the outset the Gustav's gun armament proved wholly inadequate to knock down the big American bombers, each of which possessed 10 heavy machine guns. Flying in great 'boxes' the bombers' mutual protection afforded by literally hundreds of such guns rendered impossible the task of the German fighter pilots to attack individual aircraft inside the formations, so that once more the head-on firing pass (used successfully by a few RAF squadrons in the Battle of Britain) was adopted. At least a direct hit by

Left: *the green heart insignia identify these Gustavs as belonging to* JG 54 *during a summer campaign on the Russian Front; these were the best fighters in the theatre until mid-1943*

the Gustav's single hub-mounted cannon, fired from directly ahead, which struck a bomber's cockpit could be lethal, and usually was.

Such tactics demanded exceptionally cool nerves and excellent marksmanship, while the subsequent break-away always exposed the German pilot to a veritable storm from the bomber formation's crossfire. In due course moreover the B-17G introduced a 'chin' turret under the nose to discourage these very attacks.

Various expedients were tried to remedy the Gustav's lack of hitting power. A young pilot, Leutnant Heinz Knocke of *5./JG 1*, demonstrated that by dropping a time-fused 550-lb bomb from his fighter into a Fortress formation from above it was possible to destroy one or more of the bombers without venturing within range of the defending guns; although a number of successes were gained, too much time was wasted gaining height above the bombers. Much more widely used was the 210-mm (8.3-in) rocket, two of which were carried under the Gustav's wings; fitted with a proximity fuse this large missile proved perfectly capable of destroying a Fortress even without the need for a direct hit. However the bulky rocket tubes considerably reduced the Gustav's speed and manoeuvrability so that when, quite soon, the Americans were able to send powerful escorts along with the bombers–at first P-47s and later P-51s–the otherwise excellent German interceptors found themselves at a considerable disadvantage in fighter-versus-fighter combat.

Be that as it may the *Jagdgruppen* in Germany, increased to 12 (with upwards of 450 aircraft) in August 1943 by milking other hard-pressed fronts, were taking such a heavy toll of the American bombers–each with a 10-man crew–that provision of heavy fighter escorts was not simply a priority but essential if the daylight bombing offensive was to be maintained. When on the 17th of that month the Americans tried to bomb Regensburg and Schweinfurt they were intercepted by some 300 fighters, about half of them Gustavs, and lost 60 bombers shot down and 100 others badly damaged.

On the Eastern Front, notwithstanding the depredations for home defence, the Gustav remained the most widely-used fighter throughout 1943. By mid-October the Luftwaffe's leading fighter pilot was the 22-year-old Kommandeur of *I./JG 54 <Grünherz>*, Hauptmann Walter Nowotny, the first to achieve a score of 250 victories. His own *Schwarm*, comprising Anton Döbele, Rudolf Rademacher and Karl Schnörrer (all holders of Knight's Crosses) and which shot down more then 500 aircraft in Russia, was probably the most deadly fighting foursome in history.

Too Few Fighters, too Late – Messerschmitt Bf 109K

The Gustav remained in service until the War's end, numerous sub-variants steadily advancing its performance and hitting power. Fastest was the Bf 109G-10 with a top speed of 428 mph with DB 605 engine and water injection. While many aircraft continued to use the 210-mm rockets against Allied bombers, a new cannon, the excellent 30-mm MK 108, had become increasingly available from late 1943 and while most Gustavs were armed with one such weapon in addition to their 13-mm guns, external packs of cannon were also 'bolted on'.

Spurred by the increasing toll of German fighters being taken by the American P-47s and early P-51s in

Messerschmitt Bf 109K firing a Gr 21 rocket into a box of B17s

MICHAEL TURNER
'85

1944 Messerschmitt embarked on one final production version of the 109, the 109K. This was largely based on the G-10 with DB 605 engine and an improved water injection system which boosted the power output to some 2,000 hp and the top speed to 452 mph for short bursts; armed with either a single 30-mm and two 15-mm guns, or three 30-mm and two 13-mm guns, the K version was unquestionably the most potent of all 109s, although by no means the most popular.

It entered service with some of the home defence Gruppen in September 1944 and, in experienced hands, was at least a match for the Tempest and P-47 fighters; alas for Germany the really expert fighter pilots were by then either dead or being posted to units in the process of receiving the new jet fighters. Two men however stand out even among the legendary fighter *Experten*; both flew with *JG 52* on the Eastern Front throughout 1944, 'graduating' to 109Ks in the autumn. Gerhard Barkhorn had been in Russia with *II./JG 52* since August 1942, taking command of that Gruppe in June 1943, scoring his 250th victory on February 13 the following year while flying the Gustav; when he left to command *JG 6* and ultimately to join Galland's jet-equipped *JV 44* his score was nearing 300 (he ultimately scored 301 victories).

Surpassing even Barkhorn's record, the 22-year-old Erich ('Bubi') Hartmann had always been relatively junior in the Geschwader and only rose to *Staffelkapitän* of the *4.Staffel* in October 1944 when he was allotted a K-model aircraft. He had just been awarded the Diamonds (Barkhorn 'only' received the Swords) with a score of 301 victories; between then and the end of the War his tally advanced to no less than 352 at a time when the Allies possessed almost universal air supremacy over the Reich. This score was by far the highest ever achieved by a single pilot of any nationality. Ironically he was handed over to the Russians by the Americans at the end of the War and was imprisoned for ten years on the pretext of having escaped from a Soviet POW camp in 1943!

Believing that only desperate measures could wear down the Allied pressure on Germany in the last six months of the War, the Luftwaffe undertook a number of costly adventures, all involving Bf 109Gs and Ks. In a bid to disable the Allies' forward airfields in Holland, Belgium and France, the Luftwaffe assembled about 750 fighters and fighter-bombers on bases scattered throughout Western Germany for a great attack, scheduled for dawn on New Year's Day 1945. In many instances this was to be the first operational flight by the Bf 109K pilots whose formations were led by 'pathfinder' Junkers Ju 88G night fighters. Although Operation *Bodenplatte* achieved tactical surprise and caused the destruction of some 500 Allied aircraft, none of the Allied airfields was critically damaged, and the cost was about 300 German aircraft (many of which crashed on their return flight). The RAF and American aircraft were quickly replaced from stocks, whereas the Luftwaffe's pilots were irreplaceable.

An even more poignant act of desperation was the final sortie of the so-called *Rammkommando Elbe*, a large assembly of Gustavs and 109Ks, the majority flown by pilots who in the main were fresh out of flying schools and not yet fully trained for combat. On April 7, 1945 150 aircraft took off to intercept an approaching raid by American heavy bombers, their pilots under orders to bale out after aiming their aircraft to collide with a hostile raider. This was not conceived in any way as a suicide mission (in the Japanese sense); the instigator of the plan, Oberst Hajo Herrmann—a distinguished pilot of whom more will be said in due course—had already survived two such rammings. On that April day just 15 Messerschmitts returned, but fewer than a dozen bombers had succumbed to ramming while 135 German fighters were lost.

As the final day of defeat for Germany approached, the Luftwaffe still possessed hundreds of excellent, fully airworthy fighters and the factories were still turning them out at an astonishing rate. But the once-proud and highly professional air force was to be virtually grounded, not by defeat in the air but by the destruction of the nation's fuel industry, bombed to oblivion in the last great offensives by the RAF and USAAF.

Mines and Torpedoes – Heinkel He 115

The twin-engine, twin-float Heinkel He 115 seaplane was one of those excellent pre-War German designs which, on account of a thoroughly sound and uncomplicated concept, survived in service right up to the end of the War. It was first flown in 1936 as a general purpose maritime aircraft and ordered into production the following year, equipping eleven *Staffeln* of the *Küstenfliegergruppen*.

With a crew of three (pilot, observer/gunner and navigator/bomb aimer), the He 115 was originally intended to perform bombing, mining and coastal reconnaissance duties, but soon after the outbreak of war most of the *Staffeln* became fully occupied in mining off the French and English ports. For this duty the He 115B normally carried a single 2,200-lb parachute magnetic mine but later, as the 1,940-lb weapon became available, two were often carried, these being dropped without parachute from very low altitude–an unpopular job when carried out at night as there were several instances when the mines fell on sandbanks and detonated prematurely, destroying the aircraft. Equipped with either accoustic or magnetic fuses, with or without time-delayed arming and with a nasty little anti-handling device, these mines caused heavy shipping losses until one was defused by the Royal Navy and its secrets revealed. The first such mining sorties were carried out by *Kü.Fl.Gr106* and *906* in November 1939 in the Thames Estuary and off the Essex and Suffolk coasts.

Mining of British waters by the He 115s continued throughout 1940, the total force of aircraft deployed for these duties reaching a peak of about 80, although during the Battle of Britain no fewer than 32 were lost. Seven *Staffeln* were based at Schellingwoude and Ijmuiden in Holland, Trondheim and Stavanger in Norway and at Norderney off the North German coast. An unusual task also fell to the He 115s on August 15, when Luftwaffe units based in Scandinavia joined in the great attacks: *Kü.Fl.Gr.506* flew a 'spoof' raid by 15 seaplanes towards the Scottish coast in an

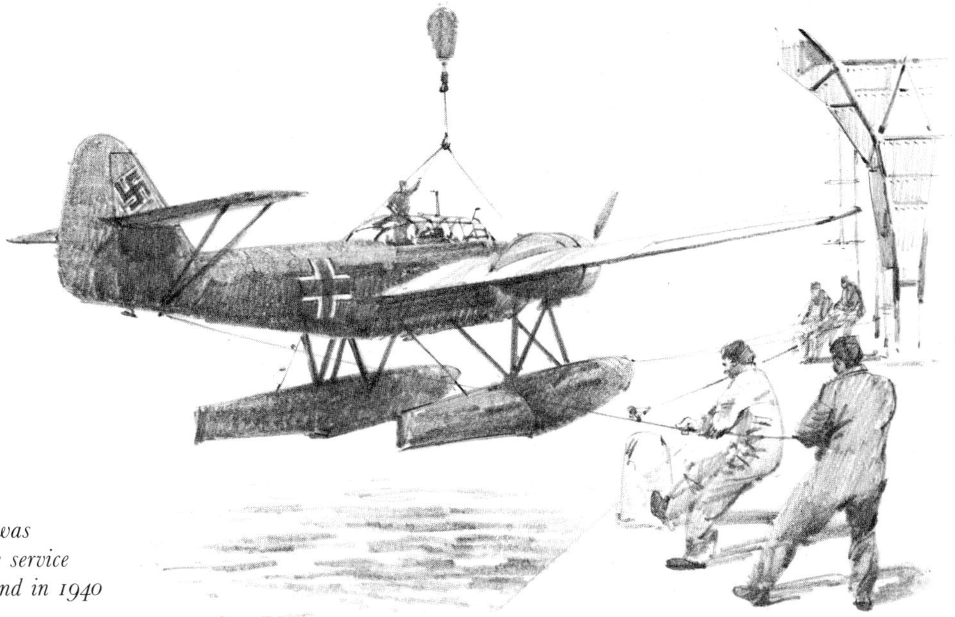

The Fokker D VIII was pressed into Luftwaffe service after the fall of Holland in 1940

A seaplane that gave excellent service was the Heinkel He 115, seen here on its beaching trolley at a Norwegian port; early in the War it undertook mining operations over the North Sea

attempt to draw off RAF fighters from a raid by *KG 26's* He 111s. Unfortunately the British failed to react; moreover the previous night one of the seaplanes had crashed into a hill near Montrose when its pilot was evidently blinded by searchlights – among the wreckage was found a map on which was marked the track of the 'spoof' raid!

The Heinkels continued to mine British ports after 1940, although on a reduced scale, as other aircraft such as the He 111 and Ju 88 were also committed to the task of preventing the movement of British merchant shipping. Indeed *Kü.Fl.Gr.106* and *506* were redesignated *Kampfgruppen 106* and *506* and re-equipped with Ju 88s.

Küstenfleigergruppe 406 however retained the He 115 and in 1941 the 115C was introduced for work in the far north, flying from bases near Tromsö, Narvik and Vadsö in Norway. Armament was increased and the undersides of the floats were reinforced to enable the aircraft to operate from snow and icefields well inside the Arctic Circle. Now that the Luftwaffe (and Kriegsmarine) had overcome stability and fusing

problems that had plagued German torpedoes early in the War, the He 115C was also employed as a torpedo bomber, and it was in this capacity that it was operated with some success against the Allied North Cape convoys. When the ill-fated PQ 17 convoy sailed in July that year an attack led by Hauptmann Eberhard Peukert, *Staffelkapitän* of *1.Staffel*, scored a hit on the American freighter *Christopher Newport*. One aircraft was hit and forced to ditch in the icy seas, but its crew was rescued when another He 115 alighted alongside.

An interesting sideline on the activities of Heinkel He 115s during the War involved their use by the RAF! Shortly before the War Germany had exported six aircraft to Norway, and during the invasion campaign of 1940 several of these were flown to Britain. Two were taken over by the RAF, one of them flying from Woodhaven near Dundee on clandestine operations with the Norwegians, carrying agents to and from their country after the German occupation; the other aircraft was flown to Malta in 1941 by Lieut Offerdahl where it was used in great secrecy to land saboteurs on the coast of North Africa behind the Axis lines.

Although production of the He 115 was halted late in 1940 to make way for production of other aircraft, and losses had almost halved the number in service by 1941, the survivors with the Luftwaffe gave such excellent service that production was re-started in 1943 when a further 141 He 115Es were produced, these giving service in the Baltic right up to the end of the War.

Corrugated Metal and Dustbins – Junkers Ju 52/3m

A German aircraft evocative of the invasion of Europe was 'Tante Ju' (Auntie Junkers), with its peculiar corrugated skin, angular lines, three engines and fixed landing gear. It was certainly one of the most-used of all Luftwaffe aeroplanes, whether it was dropping *Fallschirmjäger* (paratroops) over Norway, Holland and Crete, evacuating wounded men from Demyansk, delivering ammunition supplies to Stalingrad or carrying fuel to von Arnim's trapped divisions in Tunisia.

Developed through a long line of Professor Hugo Junkers' radical all-metal monoplanes, which started with the E I (the 'tin donkey') of 1915 and continued through a number of successful three-engine airliners in the 1920s, the Ju 52/3m was designed by Dipl Ing Ernst Zindel in 1930 and first flown with three American Pratt & Whitney Hornet radial engines in April 1932 as a commercial airliner. Although the aircraft was intended specifically for scheduled airline use by Lufthansa (which eventually received 230 examples) and numerous other carriers throughout the world, it was not long before the infant Luftwaffe expressed interest in acquiring a militarised version for use as a makeshift bomber. No fewer than 450 such aircraft, the Ju 52/3mg3e, were delivered during 1934-35. These robust but somewhat antiquated aeroplanes

Widespread use of paratroops was made during the 1940 invasion of Holland. Despite light figher opposition the Ju 52/3m Gruppen *suffered heavy casualties – principally from the flak defences*

were armed with a machine gun in an open dorsal position and another in a folding 'dustbin' suspended from the fuselage between the landing gear struts.

One of the first dedicated bomber units to receive the Ju 52/3m was *KG 152 <Hindenburg>* in 1935, and at the start of the Spanish Civil War in July the following year 20 aircraft were despatched to support the Nationalist cause. One of their first tasks was to airlift 10,000 Moorish troops from Morocco to Southern Spain, and they were joined in this task by other Ju 52/3ms supplied direct to Franco's forces. The Condor Legion, formed in November 1936 under General Hugo Sperrle, deployed the Ju 52/3ms into three *Staffeln*, and for nine months flew raids on Republican-held ports on the Mediterranean coast until replaced by Do 17s and He 111s as Soviet I-15 fighters rendered their use too risky.

In the Luftwaffe at home, bomber units which had been equipped with the Junkers were now re-termed *Kampfgruppen zur besonderen Verwendung* (*KGrzbV*), ostensibly to embrace transport duties but also, in the event of emergency, bombing. In the invasion following the Austrian *Anschluss* of March 1938 Ju 52/3ms of the *KGrzbVs* were used in large numbers to airlift the forces of occupation, and again during the seizure of the Sudetenland after the Munich Agreement. The truly massive formations of transport aircraft and bombers created exactly the desired effect for intimidation needed by the Nazis at the beginning of their territorial adventures.

Although the Luftwaffe possessed 547 Ju 52/3ms on the eve of Hitler's attack on Poland the transports were used very sparingly during that month-long campaign, and no major airborne operation was mounted. Their real baptism of fire came during Operation *Weserübung*, the invasion of Denmark and Norway in April 1940, by which time the Luftwaffe's Ju 52 inventory had been increased to 573.

In the swift elimination of Denmark a single *Staffel*, carrying 120 troops, was all that was necessary to secure the vital Vordingborg road/rail bridge linking the island of Zealand to Falster, thereby facilitating the capture of Copenhagen; other airborne troops captured the airfield at Aalborg which was immediately used by the Luftwaffe for staging north to Norway.

The paratroops of *Fallchirmjäger Regiment 1* were dropped by 24 Ju 52/3ms of *5.* and *6./KGrzbV 1* to capture Oslo-Fornebu airport, allowing reinforcements to be brought in by *KGrzbV 102*, *103* and *107*. Likewise Ju 52/3ms landed on the important airfield at Stavanger to the west, as float-equipped Ju 52/3mW (*Wasser*, or water) delivered assault troops to numerous Norwegian fjords to cut the coastal road and rail links. During the entire campaign the *KGrzbVs*, under the overall command of Oberstleutnant Carl-August Baron von Gablenz, carried 29,000 men, 2,300 tons of supplies and delivered nearly 260,000 gallons of aircraft fuel. Losses during the campaign were very heavy, 153 Ju 52/3ms being lost or written off. Among the tactics employed by the transport aircraft was the dropping of troops without parachutes from slow- and low-flying Ju 52/3ms into deep snow drifts among the Norwegian mountains (as far as is known this hazardous tactic remained unique to the 1940 campaign!).

A new element in airborne attack was introduced in the German Operation *Gelb* (Yellow), the assault in the West, which opened on May 10. Shortly before dawn that day 41 Ju 52/3ms took off from two airfields near Cologne, each towing a DFS 230 troop-carrying glider carrying eight troops from *Sturm-Abteilung Koch*, their objectives the Belgian fort of Eben-Emael and the nearby bridges over the Albert Canal. Having captured the fort the assault troops held the position until the arrival of the main ground forces 24 hours later. Elsewhere the Ju 52/3ms were used to drop paratroops at key objectives in Holland, including the Moerdijk bridges and Rotterdam's Waalhaven airport. Once more their losses–167 transports–were heavy, most of them falling to sustained and accurate flak defences.

Parachutists over Europe – Junkers Ju 52/3m

After the initial shock attacks of Operation *Gelb*, and the unexpectedly high casualties totalling well over 300 transports in Norway and the West, General Putzier, commanding the airborne forces in the Luftwaffe, withdrew the *KGrzbV* from the battle, intending to build up his strength for the planned invasion of Britain. As of course this never materialised it was not until the invasion of Greece (Operation *Marita*) of April 1941 that the ungainly Junkers transports were once more used in battle. During this operation a paratroop drop over the Corinth Canal on the 26th failed to secure its bridge objectives, but its failure little affected the outcome of the Wehrmacht's swift conquest of Greece.

In the Battle of Crete (Operation *Mercury*) the full weight of the Luftwaffe's transport resources–some 493 Ju 52/3ms and about 80 DFS 230 gliders under the command of Generalleutnant Kurt Student–was thrown into the fray. Although the loss of the island was undoubtedly a foregone conclusion for the Allies,

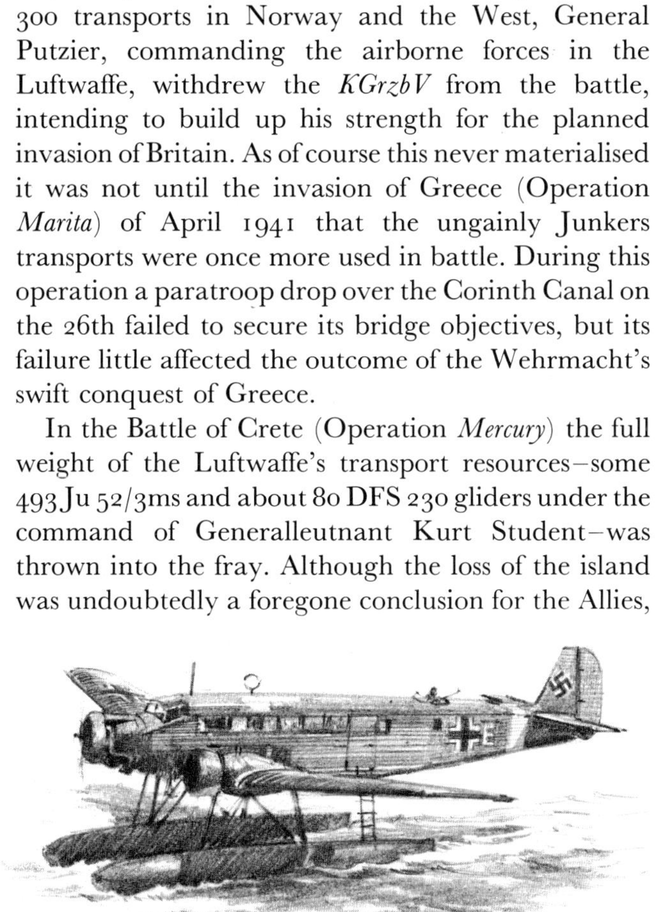

the conduct of the airborne operation was badly bungled, uncertain refuelling arrangements in Greece for the transport aircraft between the paratrooping phases leading to a disastrous lack of attack concentration. Losses among the *Fallschirmjäger* were enormous–one in every four of the paratroops being killed or wounded–while the destruction of more than a third of the transport fleet could have constituted a severe setback on the eve of Hitler's next venture, the great attack on the Soviet Union.

In the event the experiences suffered by the *Fallschirmjäger* in the Balkan campaign served simply to confirm the German High Command's suspicions that employment of paratroops, except in very small numbers against special key targets, was extremely wasteful both in men and aircraft. Accordingly none of the initial attack plans for Operation Barbarossa involved the use of airborne troops, the Wehrmacht relying solely upon the copybook Blitzkrieg tactics of old. Instead the operational *Transportverbande*, now reduced by losses to some 240 Ju 52/3ms in six Gruppen, was tasked exclusively with movement of troops and supplies behind the enormous Front. The wisdom of this decision soon became evident as the German advance started. Everywhere the Russian forces destroyed bridges, roads and railways as they fell back, so that the Wehrmacht's vehicles would have been powerless to move without a constant flow of fuel delivered forward by the transport aircraft.

That is not to suggest that all the Luftwaffe's Ju 52/3m resources were assembled in the East. By mid-1941 much of Europe had fallen under the Nazi yoke, with forces of occupation or otherwise employed in Poland, Denmark, Norway, Holland, Belgium, France, Austria, Czechoslovakia, Italy, Sicily, Sardinia, Yugoslavia, Greece, Hungary, Romania and Bulgaria. In September Finland was to join the Axis. Further afield German forces were fighting in North Africa. The large number of garrison forces thus deployed required considerable transportation, not least such isolated units dispersed among the islands of the Aegean. In every instance Ju 52/3ms were in constant use, maintaining communications with the High Command, distributing mail, fuel, medical supplies, reinforcements and the other paraphernalia of military operations. New, more powerful versions of '*Tante Ju*' had been introduced, some with heavier

'Tante Ju' was as familiar to the Wehrmacht as to the Luftwaffe. Here mountain troops carry a colleague, injured on exercise, down to a landing strip for evacuation to hospital

defensive armament, others with float gear (already mentioned) or skis. There was also even a version fitted with a large duralumin hoop energised by an auxiliary motor for exploding Allied magnetic mines; delivered to the *Minensuchsgruppe* in France, these aircraft were tasked with keeping the approaches to the Atlantic coastal U-boat bases clear of mines.

In the Mediterranean theatre early operations by the Ju 52/3ms were largely routine, embracing the ground support of front line units as well as assisting in the periodic redeployment of combat units of the Luftwaffe. When, from time to time, *Jagdgeschwader* were moved from North Africa to another front, or vice versa, ground crews, spares and tools were carried in the Junkers.

In April 1943, in the dying hours of the Axis forces in North Africa, the old Junkers suffered disaster. Assailed by British and American forces from the land, sea and air, the remnants of the Afrika Korps, now commanded by General Jürgen von Arnim, were in desperate need of supplies. Every available transport aircraft in the Mediterranean theatre was rushed to Sardinia and Sicily to carry fuel and ammunition across the Sicilian Channel. Despite efforts to provide the vulnerable Ju 52s with at least a token escort, the Allied fighters frequently descended on the hapless transports; on one occasion – 18 April – 52 out of a formation of over 100 petrol-laden Ju 52s were shot down off Cap Bon. In little over a fortnight this forlorn operation cost the Luftwaffe the loss of 432 transport aircraft. Following the appalling misfortunes that had befallen the German forces on the Eastern Front the *Transportverbande* had suffered a defeat from which it was never to recover.

Auntie Junkers to the Rescue – Ju 52/3m

It is perhaps pertinent to reflect that Germany was defeated in the East as much by the sheer distances involved as by the harsh winter conditions and the ultimate strength of the Russian forces: distances over which Wehrmacht supplies had to be transported as it advanced and distances between the front line and the main Soviet war industries which should have been destroyed – had the Luftwaffe possessed the long-range bombers to do so.

To satisfy the voracious appetite of the Wehrmacht for supplies as it moved further east the *Transportverbande* slowly expanded from the initial six Gruppen of Ju 52/3ms in June 1941 to a peak strength of 21 with all manner of impressed aircraft at the time of the Stalingrad *débâcle* 18 months later.

The first major test of the Luftwaffe's ability to sustain the Wehrmacht came in January 1942 when four Russian armies encircled six divisions, totalling 100,000 men of the *X. Armee Korps* at Demyansk, south of Leningrad. At once Oberst Friedrich Morzik, *Lufttransportführer Ost* (Commander, Air Transport, East) was ordered to supply the trapped divisions by air with such aircraft that he could muster. At the time Morzik could call on no more than 50 Ju52/3ms and about 60 makeshift He 111s in two Gruppen, capable between them of lifting about 60 tons of supplies daily. His own airfields at Korovje-Selo, Ostrov and Pskov were wholly inadequate to cope with heavily laden transports, being covered with snow and ice, while the landing area at Demyansk itself was able to accommodate no more than 40–50 aircraft arrivals each day. Moreover the Russian air force was beginning to make any movement by the slow transports extremely hazardous. Nevertheless by an extraordinary feat of organisation Morzik not only collected eight further *Gruppen* of transports by milking other fronts but succeeded in levelling and draining his own airfields and establishing a second landing area at Pyesky in the Demyansk pocket. By mid-April some 300 Ju 52 sorties were being flown to the encircled troops daily; some aircraft, with fighter protection, air-dropped supplies direct to the fighting men.

By May the Wehrmacht had fought its way through to relieve *X.Armee Korps*. Morzik's feat of hasty improvisation had enabled a total of 24,000 tons of supplies and 15,000 troops to be flown into the pocket, and 20,000 wounded to be evacuated. The transport aircraft had suffered heavily; 262 aircraft had been lost–many of them in take-off and landing accidents–and 385 aircrew killed. Morzik had himself been awarded the Knight's Cross on 16 April.

Such a triumph of improvisation nevertheless imbued the German High Command with fatal overconfidence in the capabilities of the *Transportverbande*. When on November 23 that same year another great Russian encircling movement trapped General Friedrich Paulus' *6.Armee* at Stalingrad, Göring boasted his confidence in the Luftwaffe's ability to sustain the quarter of a million troops facing annihilation, a task that would demand the delivery of at least 300 tons of supplies daily.

Certainly such a target seemed achievable, with the losses at Demyansk more than made good (more than 500 new Ju 52/3ms were built in 1942 alone); moreover large numbers of other aircraft could be impressed into service for transport work. Despite this mounting assembly of aircraft, the air bridge was desperately slow in building up, once more the appalling weather and lack of adequate landing grounds proving the limiting factors. Moreover the

Aircraft maintenance by the Luftwaffe in Russia always involved rudimentary and makeshift conditions, as demonstrated by this field blacksmith at work on the exhaust manifold of a Ju 52/3m

MICHAEL TURNER '85

Russian air force had grown immeasurably more powerful.

It has been estimated that at the beginning of the Stalingrad battle the Luftwaffe could muster about 300 Ju 52s and some 100 He 111s, of which about half were airworthy at any one time. Within a week this force was able to deliver some 100 tons in a single day to the airfields at Gumrak, Pitomnik and Tazinskaya. Three weeks later the daily average had doubled, but already the Russian armies were threatening the landing areas. On December 24 Tazinskaya fell to Soviet armoured forces, more than 100 Junkers making good their escape with only minutes to spare.

On January 16 Pitomnik was captured, the airfield littered with the wrecks of more han 60 Ju 52/3ms; at Sverevo, where most of the surviving transports were now forced to land, 52 more aircraft were destroyed in an air attack by Soviet bombers. When Gumrak fell on the 22nd the Luftwaffe could do no more than parachute supplies to the half-frozen men of *6.Armee*. Ten days later von Paulus had no alternative but to surrender.

Luftwaffe losses at Stalingrad were truly disastrous, more than 2,000 aircraft of all types being destroyed in 70 days. 315 Ju 52/3ms lay shattered on the frozen wastes, leaving about 180 such aircraft to cater to the needs of the entire Eastern Front. Henceforth however, no matter what prodigious efforts might be made to build new aircraft, the work of the venerable '*Tante Ju*' would be one of assisting the Wehrmacht to withdraw westwards–a task rendered infinitely hazardous now that superiority in the air had passed irredeemably to the enemy.

The Eyes of the Commerce Raider – Arado Ar 196

It was in 1937 that the Kriegsmarine laid plans to acquire a suitable floatplane with which to equip its new generation of ocean-going warships for purposes of reconnaissance. The future rôle of the German Navy was seen to be that of widespread commerce raiding, particularly by the so-called pocket battleships, and later by such capital ships as the *Scharnhorst* and *Gneisenau*. Hitherto a small number of Heinkel He 60 and He 114 biplanes had served at sea but it was now recognised that better speed and range performance would be needed, as well as better resistance to salt water corrosion during prolonged raiding sorties.

Accordingly four Arado Ar 196 prototypes were produced in 1938, two with the conventional twin-float arrangement and two with single central float and balancing floats under the wings. After evaluation of the two designs the former was selected for production and, with 960-hp BMW radial engine, the first Ar 196A-s were delivered to the Kriegsmarine in August 1939. These aircraft were just too late to join the pocket battleships *Deutschland* and *Admiral Graf Spee* when they sailed just before the War into the Atlantic to commence their commerce raiding.

By the end of the year 26 of the seaplanes had been completed and delivered to the Fleet Aircraft Unit, *Bordfliegergruppe 196*, and delivered to the battlecruisers *Scharnhorst* and *Gneisenau* (four aircraft each), and the pocket battleships *Admiral Scheer* and *Lützow* (ex-*Deutschland*, two aircraft each). Early in 1940 the German auxiliary commerce raiders *Atlantis* (*Schiff 16*, two aircraft), *Orion* (*Schiff 36*, two aircraft), *Widder* (*Schiff 21*, one aircraft) and *Pinguin* (*Schiff 33*, two aircraft) also took aboard the Arado seaplane.

As production continued, those aircraft of *BFGr 196* that were not embarked in naval vessels were distributed by Staffel between the various seaplane anchorages along the coasts of German-occupied Europe, their multifarious tasks including air-sea

The Kriegsmarine made constant use of seaplanes such as the excellent Arado Ar 196 seen here over the pocket battleship Lützow (*formerly the* Deutschland)

MICHAEL TURNER '85

rescue, anti-submarine patrol and escort for German coastal shipping. Early in 1940 a new version, the Ar 196A-3 appeared with a pair of 20-mm cannon in the wings, and it was in one such aircraft that Leutnant Günther Mehrens of *Küstenfliegergruppe 706* spotted the British minelaying submarine HMS *Seal* disabled on the surface in the Kattegat on 5 May that year; attacking with cannon and light bombs Mehrens forced the British submarine captain, Lieut-Cdr Rupert Lonsdale, to surrender his boat.

Meanwhile the auxiliary commerce raider *Atlantis* had sailed from Kiel on March 11 and steamed north disguised as a Russian merchant ship. Altering course to the west and then south through the Denmark Strait into the Atlantic she then began the most successful of all raiding voyages by any German surface vessel during the War, her two Arado seaplanes being employed to scout beyond her horizons for Allied shipping. Often she would not bother to attack ships sailing in ballast, any transmission of 'raider reports' serving her purpose of causing the greatest disruption to British convoy sailings and distraction of escort vessels. In the course of 30 weeks at sea in the Atlantic, Indian and Pacific Oceans the *Atlantis* sank 22 ships totalling 145,697 tons, her aircraft also being used on occasion to discourage the victims from using their radios by shooting up the wireless cabin and transmitter aerials. She was eventually sunk by the cruiser HMS *Devonshire* near Ascension Island on November 22 while refuelling a U-boat when neither of her Arados was serviceable. Her crew was rescued by the U-boat and brought home to Germany where her captain, Kapitän-zur-See Bernhard Rogge, received the Knight's Cross and later the Oakleaves.

During the Battle of Britain Ar 196s were active in all the waters round the British Isles, *1./BFGr 196* being based initially at Schellingwoude but later at Boulogne and Cherbourg (losing four aircraft in a severe storm which lashed the anchorage at Cherbourg on October 1, 1940). Several were shot down by RAF fighters, and on one occasion an Arado pilot strayed too close to a Royal Navy vessel, mistaking the Ensign for a Red Cross flag, and was shot down for his pains. On August 5 the heavy cruisers *Admiral Hipper*, on a raiding sortie off the Greenland coast, lost one of her three Ar 196s when it crashed while trying to alight in heavy seas.

When the battleship *Bismarck* was being hunted by British ships and aircraft in the North Atlantic the following year all four of her Ar 196A-3s were flown off to try to discourage the shadowing Catalina flying boats, a desperate act in view of the likely time taken to recover the seaplanes at the end of their sorties. Equipping several *Seeaufklärungsgruppen* (maritime reconnaissance groups) on the French Atlantic seaboard, Ar 196s were used in growing numbers in 1942 to escort U-boats returning to port, and several RAF flying boats and other aircraft were shot down by the seaplanes' cannon. Indeed this very popular and useful aeroplane continued in service with shorebased units almost up to the end of the War, a total of 593 being produced, including a small number of examples built by the French and Dutch for the Luftwaffe.

To Destroy or be Destroyed – Messerschmitt Bf 110

The *Zerstörer* (destroyer) concept of heavy fighter, exemplified in its first generation by the twin-engine two-seat Messerschmitt Bf 110, was largely a relic of General Wever's vision of a strategically-tasked Luftwaffe for, believing that Germany's bombers needed to be able to strike targets anywhere in Europe, he considered a necessary adjunct to this to be a long-range escort fighter. When design work started in 1934 the all-metal Bf 110 was an exceptionally advanced aircraft, being intended to use the new Daimler Benz DB 600 engines. When it first flew in May 1936 it proved very fast indeed and, although plans for a strategic bomber force had been scrapped, it entered production in 1938 with an armament of two 20-mm cannon and four 7.9-mm machine guns in the nose, and a single machine gun in the rear cockpit.

The first major service version was the Bf 110C-series which joined the Luftwaffe in February 1939 powered by two 1,100-hp DB 601A engines and possessing a top speed of slightly over 350 mph. There is no doubt that on paper the new *Zerstörer* was indeed a formidable aeroplane, so much so that Göring himself initiated the creation of a new fighter arm in the Luftwaffe, the *Zerstörerverbande* and forthwith directed that the best fighter pilots be posted to these units. In truth no one was entirely clear as to what the new fighters were to do, other than to provide escorts for the Luftwaffe's bombers. When the first Bf 110Cs joined *I.(Zerstörer)/LG 1*–a sort of operational

development unit – they were flown by many pilots who had previous experience on the nimble Bf 109C and D, and who now began to question the Bf 110's ability to dogfight with interceptors – a doubt that had been previously expressed but brushed aside.

When Germany went to war in 1939 the Luftwaffe possessed just under 200 Bf 110s, of which about 80 were in service with *I./ZG 1* commanded by the one-legged First World War veteran Major Joachim-Friedrich Huth, and I./ZG 76 under Hauptmann Reinecke, deployed against Poland. The shortlived and disastrously one-sided Polish campaign featured very few conclusive combats with the *Zerstörer*, and it was the clash with RAF Wellingtons over the Heligoland Bight on 18 December 1939 (when 12 out of 22 bombers were shot down) that lent weight to Göring's belief in the *Zerstörer's* invincibility.

How wrong he was proved to be was shown all too clearly in the Battle of Britain, by which time the Bf 110 was already beginning to be used as a fighter-bomber, as well as in the escort fighter rôle. By mid-July a total of 220 Bf 110s was deployed in eight Gruppen in France with about 30 others with *I./ZG 76*

Possessing high speed the Bf 110 Zerstörer *was nevertheless no match for the RAF's nimble interceptors. Here Hurricanes attack an He 111 formation with Bf 109 and 110 escorts over the Channel in 1940*

at Stavanger in Norway. From the outset the *Zerstörergruppen* were tasked with escorting the bomber formations in raids over Southern England, but the RAF soon found that the Hurricane–normally sent against the bombers, leaving the Spitfires to deal with the German fighters–was perfectly capable of outfighting the *Zerstörer*. The first major battle with the Bf 110 was fought over the South Coast on August 11 when six of *I./ZG 2's* aircraft were shot down, including that of the *Gruppenkommandeur*, Major Ott. It was however during the heavy fighting on the 15th that the *Zerstörergeschwader* suffered their heaviest casualties: on 'Black Thursday' *ZG 76* lost 19 aircraft together with two group commanders; eight other Bf 110s were also shot down. Thereafter the ridiculous and highly unpopular expedient was adopted of providing the *Zerstörer* formations with their own escorts of Bf 109Es!

Dismal though these events must have been to the *Zerstörer* units (no fewer than 263 Bf 110s were lost in combat during the Battle of Britain), one unit in particular served the Luftwaffe well. Formed early in July to evolve fighter-bomber tactics in combat conditions with the Bf 110, *Erprobungsgruppe 210* was commanded by the 30-year-old Swiss pilot, Hauptmann Walter Rubensdörffer. His *1.* and *2.Staffeln* were equipped with bomb-carrying Bf 110s while *3.Staffel* flew Bf 109E single-seaters, also mounting a single 250-kg bomb. His objectives were invariably chosen as being key targets–main airfields, radar stations, fighter factories and the like–and his tactics were to send the Bf 109s in first to drop their bombs and then provide top cover while the 110s swept in to deliver their bombs. Not surprisingly Rubensdörffer's targets were heavily defended and casualties were high. The Swiss pilot was himself shot down and killed on August 15 when his formation was set upon by Hurricanes after a low level raid on Croydon. Both his successors in command were shot down in turn during the Battle. In due course *Erpr.Gr 210's* rôle changed to one of daylight pathfinding, the Bf 110s' crews being briefed to lead large formations of Heinkel He 111s and Junkers Ju 88s against such targets as the Bristol aircraft and engine factories, the intention being to mark the target with bombs for the benefit of the 'main force'. This tactic seldom succeeded for the RAF fighters usually went straight for the bomb-laden Bf 110s which had to jettison their loads in order to defend themselves. The Battle of Britain virtually killed the idea of using the Bf 110 as an escort fighter, and henceforth it came to be used as a fighter-bomber, particularly in conditions of German air superiority.

Scene typical of Zerstörer *operations in the Western Desert, with Bf 110s clustered around the Staffel ops tent; such desert airstrip conditions were unavoidable owing to the constant advances and withdrawals*

After the Battle of Britain – Messerschmitt Bf 110

Although air fighting remained a secondary rôle by day for the *Zerstörergeschwader*, and returned as a prime responsibility in 1943, much greater emphasis was placed on the ground support aspect of the Bf 110's capabilities after the Battle of Britain. Moreover, as many of these aircraft were now to be committed to the night fighting rôle, the number of Gruppen equipped with the *Zerstörer* declined.

In the German campaign in the Balkans in April 1941 (Operation *Strafgereit* followed by Operation *Marita*) the Luftwaffe committed a balanced force of fighters and bombers of *Luftflotte 4*, including almost 100 Bf 110s of *Zerstörergeschwader 26* <*Horst Wessel*>, led by the Battle of Britain veteran Oberst Johann Schalk who had brought his *III.Gruppe* through a number of particularly hazardous missions in August 1940 and had been awarded the Knight's Cross. One of the unit's busiest days during the Greek campaign was April 20 when a dawn attack at Gruppe strength on the British-occupied airfield at Menidi took the

defences entirely by surprise and resulted in the destruction on the ground of a dozen Blenheims. In the afternoon the entire Geschwader was ordered to escort a force of Junkers Ju 88s in a raid over Piraeus. Intercepted by 15 Hurricanes of the RAF's Nos 33 and 80 Squadrons, a prolonged air battle developed in which three Bf 110s were lost and five Hurricanes shot down; among the pilots to fall to *ZG 26's* guns was the South African Sqn Ldr M. T. St. J. Pattle, highest-scoring RAF pilot in the Second World War.

ZG 26 continued in action throughout the subsequent Battle of Crete, suffering fairly heavy casualties in the confused series of operations both against the island defenders and against ships of the Royal Navy. On May 14 the Bf 110s turned their attention to attacks on the island's airfields, being afforded protection by Bf 109s. As most of the defending Hurricanes took off and engaged the 109s the 110s of *III./ZG 26* concentrated on shooting up the airfield's defences and in one such attack on a battery of Bofors guns Oberleutnant Sophus Baagoe, who had already gained a creditable tally of 14 victories, was shot down and killed; the posthumous award of the Knight's Cross was announced exactly one month later, together with a similar award to Hauptmann Ralph von Rettburg, *Kommandeur* of *II./ZG 26*. On May 21, as German paratroops and gliders descended on Maleme airfield, British fighters engaged 27 Bf 110s of *I./ZG 26*, shooting down and killing the *Gruppenkommandeur*, Major Wilhelm Makrocki, another veteran of the Battle of Britain. His place was to be taken by one of the greatest of all *Zerstörer* pilots, Major Wilhelm Spies, who had fought in Spain, was also to win the Knight's Cross for his fighting over Crete and was to be awarded the Oakleaves posthumously after his death on the Russian Front less than a year hence. Based at Argos in Greece *ZG 26* was ordered on 22 May to escort a large force of bombers and dive bombers to attacks on ships of the Royal Navy to the west of Crete; in the attacks that followed the cruisers HMS *Fiji* and *Gloucester* were sunk, the battleship HMS *Warspite* damaged and the destroyer HMS *Greyhound* sunk.

Immediately after the battle of Crete *ZG 26* was moved, first to Sicily and then to the Eastern Front. At that time only one other ground support unit, *Schnellkampfgeschwader 210* (Fast Bomber Wing 210, which had been formed with the survivors of *Erpr.Gr 210* after the Battle of Britain), was still equipped with the Bf 110E, a recently-introduced dedicated fighter-bomber. While *SKG 210* remained in the East, *ZG 26* returned to the Central Mediterranean before being moved back to Germany for daylight defence of the Reich against the increasing American daylight raids in 1943.

By then the *Zerstörerverbande* had been considerably strengthened once more to comprise six Gruppen, namely *II./ZG 1* led by Hauptmann Egon Albrecht, the three Gruppen of *ZG 26* commanded by Major Karl Boehm-Tettelbach and two Gruppen of *ZG 76* under Major Theodor Rossiwall. Often equipped with four underwing 21-cm rockets in addition to their cannon and machine gun armament the Bf 110s made excellent bomber-destroyers prior to the introduction of American fighter escorts for their bombers, and even when the first relatively short-range P-47s arrived units such as *ZG 26* and *ZG 76*, based deep inside Germany, simply waited until the escort turned for home at the limit of its range before launching their rockets. Even if these weapons failed to knock down a bomber every time they served to break up the tight American formations so that the stragglers could be picked off by other fighters. These tactics were so effective towards the end of 1943 that American losses were seriously delaying the build-up of the daylight bombing offensive.

By early 1944 however, the Americans were introducing long range fuel tanks to enable their fighters to penetrate deep into Europe, and soon showed just what the P-47 and P-51 could do against the aging Zerstörer. The crippling losses now being suffered by the *Zerstörerverbande* now hastened the withdrawal of the survivors from the daylight battle, their place being taken by the much-improved Messerschmitt Me 410.

Jazz at Night – Messerschmitt Bf 110

Unlike the RAF, which had allocated a small number of Blenheim squadrons specifically for night defence shortly before the War and was already experimenting with rudimentary airborne radar, the Luftwaffe only began to take steps to create the semblance of a night fighter force partway through the Battle of France when British bombers started dropping bombs on German soil instead of leaflets. By June 1940 six *Staffeln*, equipped with an assortment of Bf 110Cs and Do 17Zs, of *Jagdgeschwader 1* and *Zerstörergeschwader 1* were dotted about airfields in Germany and Holland, their tactics being confined to roaming the night skies on the look out for any bomber caught in searchlights. In July these six units were amalgamated to form the first night fighter Wing, *Nachjagdgeschwader 1*, commanded by Major Wolfgang Falck, the *I.Gruppe* being equipped with Bf 110Cs and Ds (including a number of experimental 110D-0(N)s which featured an infra-red sensing device) and the *II.Gruppe* with a mixed complement of Ju 88 *Zerstörer* and Do 17Zs tasked with carrying out intruder operations over Britain.

Early in September 1940 *II./NJG 1* broke away to provide the nucleus of *NJG 2* which would henceforth concentrate on intruder work, leaving the night defence to NJG 1. Falck can be said to have been the pioneer of German night fighting tactics, quickly expanding his Wing to 10 *Staffeln*, and employing Bf 109Es as 'targets' for practising night interceptions with the infra-red device. However, early in October, he lost one of his key men when Hauptmann Graf Stillgried (*Gruppenkommandeur* of a new *II.Gruppe*) crashed in a Bf 110D-0(N) at Könen; attention then switched to work on airborne radar, in which field Germany lagged far behind Britain. In the meantime Oberst Josef Kammhuber had been ordered by Göring to establish a chain of ground radar stations extending from Denmark to Switzerland, based on pairs of what came to be known as Giant *Würzburg* stations, one of which tracked the bomber target and the other tracked and passed information to the night fighter. For this work the Bf 110 proved most suitable, the two-man crew and relatively high speed being needed while chasing British bombers all over Germany and the Low Countries at night, often in poor weather.

By mid-1941 five *Nachtjagdgeschwader* (*NJG 1* to *5*) had been formed, all but *NJG 2* flying Bf 110Cs, still without radar. By now a number of pilots had emerged as outstanding night fighters, all with *NJG 1*. Hauptmann Werner Streib (who had been officially credited with the Luftwaffe's first night victory on July 20, 1940 while flying a Bf 110C), now led *I./NJG 1* and headed the field with 15 night victories, although Oberleutnant Helmut Lent, *Staffelkapitän* of 6./*NJG 1*, had shot down 14 aircraft at night and eight by day; Oberleutnant Paul Gildner had scored 14 night victories, and Oberleutnant Reinhard Knacke, leader of *3./NJG 1*, was credited with 12.

Visual night interceptions–albeit with control instructions from the ground radar stations –continued throughout 1941. However in August that year the Telefunken company started work on its *Lichtenstein* airborne radar and by mid-1942 almost all the night fighters were radar-equipped. Until the end of the War developments in radar and radar countermeasures became a war within a war as each side strove to render its opponent's equipment useless. German night fighters began to take a substantial toll of British bombers. In 1942 RAF Bomber Command lost 1,291 aircraft in night attacks, of which roughly 800 were shot down by the Bf 110 which, by the end of the year, constituted more than three-quarters of Germany's night fighter force.

The defenders suffered a major setback on July 24, 1943 when the RAF first used a relatively simple jamming device. Codenamed Window, consisting of thousands of metal foil strips and scattered by the bombers, these blanketed the German radar screens

Festooned with radar aerials on nose and wings, a Messerschmitt Bf 110G night fighter makes ready to take off for a sortie against an RAF heavy bomber stream

with spurious signals. In this, the first of the terrible raids on Hamburg, both the *Würzburg* and *Lichtenstein* radars were rendered virtually useless. In due course however alternative tactics were introduced, including the broadcast of a commentary on the general location of the bomber stream which enabled the night fighters to navigate to a position whence to attack visually. Armament of the Bf 110 was progressively increased, and in the late summer of 1943 the first examples of a deadly armament installation–known as *Schräge Musik*, literally 'Jazz Music'–were in service. Comprising a pair of *upward* firing cannon, it enabled the night fighter to attack British bombers from underneath–invariably unseen by their crews. Indeed the RAF remained unaware of this new gun installation, despite fast accelerating loss rates. On the very first night of its use in combat on August 17, 1943, Leutnant Peter Eberhardt of *5./NJG 5* shot down four heavy bombers in 30 minutes. Such achievements were to become commonplace, and were often exceeded during the remainder of the War whenever the RAF sent bombers in strength to raid Germany. Men such as Major Heinz-Wolfgang Schnaufer, *Kommodore* of *NJG 4* with 121 night victories, and Oberst Helmut Lent, now *Kommodore* of *NJG 3* (110 victories) became legendary names throughout Germany. Truly the Bf 110 attoned at night over Germany for its failures in daylight in the Battle of Britain!

To See Over the Hill – Henschel Hs 126

In its principal task of supporting the Wehrmacht, the Luftwaffe was from its earliest days preoccupied in evolving suitable 'battlefield' aircraft, not least for short-range reconnaissance–in effect the latterday equivalent of the 'corps reconnaissance' machine of the First World War. Two such aircraft, the Heinkel He 45 biplane and He 46 high-wing monoplane, served the new air force well during the fledgling years of 1934–38, the latter even surviving in small numbers to be used during the Polish campaign of 1939. In 1936 Dipl Ing Friedrich Nicolaus at the Henschel company started work on a development of that manufacturer's own Hs 122, which had failed to enter production.

The new Henschel Hs 126 was a contemporary of the British Westland Lysander, conceived for exactly the same function. It first flew late in 1936, and appeared on the production lines in the Henschel factories at Schönefeld and Johannisthal in 1938, the first joining the Luftwaffe later that year. Six Hs 126A-1s were sent to Spain where they equipped a *Kette* of the Condor Legion's *Aufklärungsstaffel 88*, replacing the aged He 45 and giving excellent service in the final stages of the Civil War.

At home in Germany the Hs 126A-1 was first delivered to *Heeresaufklärungsgruppe 35* (Army Reconnaissance Group 35) and in 1939, with Bramo radial in the Hs 126B in place of the former BMW engine, started equipping most of the short-range reconnaissance units. By the outbreak of War 257 aircraft had been delivered to 10 *Gruppen*, each of which then comprised between three and six *Staffeln*. During the Wehrmacht's operations in 1939–40 it was customary to allocate a *Kette* of Hs 126s to a specific Army unit, a *Staffel* to a Panzer Korps and single aircraft to an artillery regiment. When working with the Wehrmacht in combat the duties of the *Heeresaufklärungsstaffeln* were denoted by '*Panzer*' and '*Artillerie*' (for example, *1.(H)/13 (Pz)* and *3.(H)/10(Art)* <*Tannenberg*>).

As the German tides of invasion rolled through Europe Henschel Hs 126s were seldom far from the advancing tank columns, on the look-out for likely points of resistance; in instances when an enemy gun battery or tanks were spotted in the path of advance the Henschel pilot would attempt to mark the position with a light bomb, as the ground vehicles were seldom in touch with the aircraft by radio. Equally often the Henschels would be sent out to reconnoitre an area of advance beforehand, their observers (*Beobachter*) delivering undeveloped film from their hand-held cameras–usually the Rb 12.5/9X7–direct to the unit command post immediately on landing.

Among the Gruppen to distinguish themselves in the Norwegian campaign of 1940 was *Aufkl.Gr 10* <*Tannenberg*> which performed extraordinary feats of reconnaissance at very low level over the mountainous territory. All available Gruppen were to participate in the Battle of France during May and June that year, there being numerous instances of Hs 126 pilots 'buzzing' large groups of refugees in attempts to encourage them to leave the roads in the path of oncoming Panzers. On one occasion a pilot dropped a light bomb in a field nearby to lend emphasis to his meaning, only to have to watch as the leading tank gunner opened fire, believing the bomb to indicate a hostile gun battery. During the Battle of Britain six *Aufklärungsstaffeln* with Henschels were moved up to the Channel Coast in France, the aircraft being used to keep watch for Frenchmen attempting to escape in small boats to England. At least one over-enthusiastic pilot ventured too close to the Kent coast and was promptly shot down by British fighters.

In 1941 two *Staffeln* were sent to Libya, *4.(H)/Aufkl.Gr 12* and *2.(H)/14*, but their Henschels were not ideal for desert operations although the removal of the wheel spats (an expedient universally adopted) did prevent sand from clogging the landing gear. They also proved extremely vulnerable as the British desert forces invariably radioed for an RAF fighter to come and deal with the intruder. The Lysander was equally vulnerable, and it was not uncommon for the reconnaissance aircraft of both sides to be provided with strong fighter escorts. Both sides got rid of the slow aeroplanes by mid-1942 as reconnaissance fighters became available.

The Henschel Hs 126B gave almost two years' yeoman service on the Russian Front, *Aufkl.Gr 41* distinguishing itself at the time of the Demyansk crisis; its aircraft were daubed with white emulsion as makeshift snow camouflage, while most of the Hs 126s were temporarily fitted with ski landing gear.

Gradually however the army co-operation/ reconnaissance *Gruppen* began re-equipping with the twin-engined Focke-Wulf Fw 189 which, although less suited to the task of low-level battlefield surveillance, was slightly less vulnerable to the depredations of

MICHAEL TURNER '85

Battlefield reconnaissance. Flying over one of the massive Maginot Line forts, the observer of this Aufkl.Gr 10 <Tannenberg> *Hs 126A-1 leans out of his cockpit to operate his hand-held camera*

Russian fighters, and certainly afforded better protection for the crew from the vicious winter flying weather. The Hs 126 was also used as a light glider tug with the *Luftlandegeschwader* (Air Landing Wing), towing the DFS 230, but most of the survivors were delivered to the *Nachtschlachtgruppen* for night harassing operations behind the Russian front line; the aircraft assigned to *2./NSGr 12* in Latvia eventually ended up towing gunnery targets with *Zielstaffel 10* at Riga in 1944.

On the Fringes of Europe – Blohm und Voss Bv 138

When the Blohm und Voss shipbuilding company of Hamburg opened an aircraft department in 1933 it was perhaps natural that the company embarked on the design of flying boats, although the need to provide aircraft for long-range ocean patrol had not been foreseen during the earliest planning of the Luftwaffe. In due course a radical three-engine configuration was selected and a private venture (albeit with encouragement from the RLM) was undertaken in 1935. The new aircraft, the Bv 138, featured a shoulder-wing with gull centre section and short hull, the tail unit being carried on twin booms attached to the wing; two of the engines were mounted in the front of the booms and the third centrally over the wing. Two prototypes were flown in 1937 but early trials indicated that the designers had 'got it all wrong': the short hull and broad-chord wings gave rise to marked porpoising on the water while aerodynamic lateral instability both in the air and on the water required coarse use of differential engine throttling.

A complete re-design was undertaken, involving enlarging the hull by almost 50 per cent, enlarging the tail booms and eliminating the gull wing centre section. The result was an aeroplane of exceptionally graceful if radical appearance. Twenty-five Bv 138A-1s were ordered in 1939 and the first two were flown in April 1940, just as the Norwegian campaign was starting. So short of seaplanes was the Luftwaffe however that these two aircraft were rushed into service as transports, up to 10 troops being carried by each.

When the remainder of the first batch entered service in France for patrols over the Bay of Biscay it was discovered that a number of component failures (particularly in the wings) were occurring after relatively little service. The next 21 aircraft, Bv 138B-1s, which equipped all three Staffeln of *Seeaufklärungsgruppe 130*, featured local strengthening and an increased defensive armament of two 20-mm cannon in bow and stern turrets; three 110-lb bombs could be carried under the starboard wing root.

The structural weaknesses had still not been cured, so *SAGr 130* was taken off operations for six months. By June it was flying once more, now with the Bv 138C-1. It had been discovered that the positioning of the three engines, and more particularly the plane of their propeller arcs, gave rise to a destructive resonance, to cure which simply required a different propeller on the centre engine; thus the C-series boats were fitted with one four-blade propeller and two three-blade propellers. Its troubles ended (although local strengthening continued to be carried out periodically, especially to the wing floats which came in for severe stresses in heavy seas), the Bv 138C-1 gave excellent service, 227 of this version being produced by 1943. They served with a total of 18 Staffeln of the *Küstenfliegergruppen* and *Seeaufklärungsgruppen* in Norway and the Baltic, over the Atlantic, Mediterranean and Black Sea. It was a Bv 138 of *Kü.Fl.Gr 406* based in Northern Norway whose crew, on patrol off Jan Mayen Island, first sighted the North Cape convoy PQ 18 *en route* for Russian ports in September 1942, the last such convoy to be heavily attacked by the Luftwaffe.

Bv 138Cs were equipped for catapult launching when required and those Staffeln operating from the confined waters of Norwegian fjords enjoyed the services of the catapult-equipped seaplane tender *Bussard* (Buzzard). Some of the older Bv 138Bs were modified up to 'C'-standard and joined the *Minensuchgruppen* for sea-mine detonating work off Norway and in the Mediterranean, equipped with the familiar dural hoop; in this guise–with all armament removed–the aircraft was designated the Bv 138MS (for *Minensuch*). When loaded with maximum fuel, which gave a range of some 2,600 miles, the flying boat could be fitted with a pair of assisted take-off rockets of up to 3,300-lb thrust for 30 seconds; after use the rockets were jettisoned and recoverable for further use.

In the latter stages of the War this fine workhorse set about anti-shipping operations in co-operation with U-boats in the Atlantic, being equipped with long-range *Hohentwiel* search radar. The flying boats serving in the Black Sea were pressed into service to assist in the evacuation of the Crimea, losing at least three of their number to Soviet fighters. Their final operations in the Baltic, also as evacuation transports, was fairly spectacular, it being recorded that a dozen of the flying boats carried more than 3,000 people from the north Polish ports back to Germany in little over one month, often flying in fog or at night to escape the attention of Soviet coastal vessels.

A Blohm und Voss Bv 138 takes off from a harbour in the Baltic to keep watch for Russian naval vessels operating from the island base of Kronstadt

The Wonder Bomber – Junkers Ju 88

The Junkers Ju 88 was without doubt one of the outstanding German aircraft of the War, proving as adaptable in somewhat different categories as the British Mosquito. Designed to a rather blurred requirement in 1934-35 for a *Kampfzerstörer*, or 'destroyer-bomber', it was first flown in 1936 and started to enter service with the Luftwaffe in 1939, shortly before the outbreak of war. Though mistakenly classified as a dive bomber by the Allies, on account of the 'dive brakes' under the wings, the Ju 88 was seldom used for steep dive attacks, more often approaching its target in a shallow dive so as to achieve high speed over the defended area. Such attack tactics became familiar throughout Northern Europe in the first two years of the War, beginning with a raid by *I./KG 30* <*Adler-Geschwader*> (Eagle Wing) on Royal Navy ships in the Firth of Forth on October 16, 1939, when one of the machines was the first German aircraft to be shot down on British soil during the Second World War. In the Battle of Britain Ju 88s seldom flew with escorting fighters on account of their own relatively high speed, and were initially considered to be difficult aircraft to shoot down, except when forced to fly slower by other aircraft in the formation. There were however occasions when Ju 88 formations were severely mauled, such as the raid of August 12 against targets on the English South Coast by all three Gruppen of *KG 51* <*Edelweiss*> when 10 aircraft including that of the *Geschwaderkommodore*, Oberst Dr Johann-Volkmar Fisser, were shot down; a raid on Tilbury Docks in London by *III./KG 77* on September 18 when the Ju 88 of the *Gruppenkommandeur*, Major Max Kless, was among nine out of 30 Ju 88s shot down; and the attack by *I.* and *II./KG 77* on London on September 27 which cost the loss of 12 aircraft.

Ju 88s served on every front in Europe and North Africa during the War in a variety of rôles but, until the Luftwaffe dropped all pretence at trying to sustain any sort of autonomous bombing arm in 1944, it was as a bomber and night fighter that it excelled. *KG 30* had, since the beginning of the War, been a specialist anti-shipping unit, the distinction being drawn by the form of attack: several aircraft attacked a single vessel in close line astern so as to overwhelm the gun defences. For this reason *III./KG 30's* Ju 88s (together with those of *I./LG 1*) accompanied *VIII.Fliegerkorps* for the invasion of Greece and Crete in anticipation of concerted interference by ships of the Royal Navy. It was an attack on the Piraeus harbour by the aircraft of *7./KG 30* that featured the second amazing escape from death by Hauptmann Hajo Herrmann, its *Staffelkapitän*. Herrmann's bombs struck the freighter *Clan Frazer*, which happened to have 250 tons of explosives aboard. The vessel blew up with such force that 10 other ships and much of the harbour were destroyed; the offending Ju 88 escaped only to be hit by fire from a surviving Bofors gun, causing Herrmann to make a force landing on the Italian-held island of Rhodes. (Herrmann's previous escape had been during the Battle of Britain when, letting down at night to mine Plymouth harbour, his aircraft came to rest on top of a barrage balloon; in the nick of time the Ju 88 'fell off' and Herrmann was able to regain control and bring his aircraft safely home.) *KG 30* reassembled once more in Northern Norway after the Greek campaign and was in constant action against the North Cape convoys, particularly PQ 13, 16, 17 and 18. In the most devastating of these battles the Ju 88s (once more

Of all the aircraft that attacked Malta's Grand Harbour at Valletta, the Ju 88 posed the greatest threat as it was usually able to outdistance the RAF's defending Hurricanes

MICHAEL TURNER '85

involving Herrmann, now *Gruppenkommandeur* of *III./KG 30*) sank six ships of the ill-fated PQ 17 and damaged two others.

In Russia the Ju 88 bomber units were also heavily employed and in a manner more in keeping with their intended rôle. However Göring could not resist sending his bombers 'Blitz-style' against centres of population, and the launching of Barbarossa was marked by three raids by more than 100 bombers, mostly He 111s but also four Staffeln of Ju 88As from *KG 3* and *KG 4*, on Moscow itself. Thereafter, what had been heralded as Germany's 'wonder bomber' was frequently used in penny packets against such targets as airfields and bridges – a pattern of operations that was to last for about two years. Later on, armed with guns of up to 50-mm calibre, the Ju 88P was used as a tank-buster, and various versions were also developed to enable the Ju 88 to carry torpedoes, these being used operationally in the Mediterranean.

And, as if to underline Germany's disenchantment with conventional bombers in 1944, redundant Ju 88As were converted for use as guided bombs in the extraordinary *Mistel* (Mistletoe) programme. With the nose packed with explosives, the unmanned bomber was 'flown' by the pilot of a fighter – usually a Bf 109 or Fw 190 – mounted on top, pick-a-back fashion; on reaching the target area the pilot released the Ju 88 which through radio link was guided towards its intended impact point. In the final nine months of the War a large number of attacks against targets such as bridges and tank concentrations were launched (although a major attack on the British naval base at Scapa Flow was abandoned). It was an act of desperation that did little to affect the War's final outcome, and a sad epitaph for a fine aeroplane.

Toasting Forks Over the Burning Reich – Junkers Ju 88

In much the same manner that the Mosquito was adapted as a night fighter early in its life, the Junkers Ju 88 entered service at the beginning of the War as a *Zerstörer*, the Ju 88C having a speed performance comparable to that of the Bf 110, but a range more than twice as great. Although early Ju 88Cs were flown experimentally during the Polish campaign it was not until mid-1940 that tactics had been worked out for the daylight use of the Ju 88 *Zerstörer*, it then becoming customary to 'mix in' a number of Ju 88Cs with a bomber formation, thereby disguising an escort element within a raid. Such tactics were adopted by *KG 30* in its raid by 50 aircraft on Driffield airfield on August 15; on that occasion however eight Ju 88s were shot down by RAF fighters without loss – six of them *Zerstörer*!

By then however the idea of using the Ju 88C as a night intruder had reached practical form by the creation of *II./NJG 1* (later to become *NJG 2*). Based at Gilze-Rijen in Holland, its aircraft took off to operate singly at night in the vicinity of RAF bomber bases in Lincolnshire and East Anglia, in the hope of attacking aircraft as they returned from raids. Bearing in mind that these early Ju 88s possessed no radar the results achieved in 1940 by the intruders were extremely promising, a total of 31 Wellingtons, Hampdens, Hudsons and Whitleys being shot down for the loss of four Ju 88Cs in combat (another being lost in a night landing accident).

Further development of the Ju 88C as a 'night destroyer' continued in 1941 and 1942, the various *Lichtenstein* radars becoming available in the latter year, The year 1943 brought the more powerful Ju 88R which carried even more extensive radar, a bewildering array of aerials sprouting on the nose, wings and tail of the night fighters, culminating in the efficient *Lichtenstein SN-2*. Untidiest of all was the *Hirschgeweih* 'toasting fork' aerial array for the *Neptun V* radar.

At the beginning of 1944 the Ju 88G night fighter started appearing, effectively the definitive night fighter version of this excellent aircraft, its long range performance being particularly important in enabling the fighter to remain 'concealed' within a bomber stream as its pilot stalked about, picking off unwary crews as they approached their target or relaxed on the way home.

By 1944 German night fighting tactics had reached a very high pitch of efficiency, a whole catalogue of alternative expedients having been evolved to counter the growing number of ways in which the RAF could interfere with Luftwaffe radar and radio communications. To begin with the Germans had produced a radar which could detect the RAF bombing radar (H2S) as soon as the sets were switched on before the bombers even left the English coast, thereby providing early warning that a raid was approaching and enabling Luftwaffe night fighters to assemble at their pre-arranged beacons. Once inside the bomber stream the RAF's use of 'Window' merely confirmed the proximity of bombers, and some Ju 88Gs even carried radar that would home on to the Lancaster's tail warning radar. Once more the deadly *Schräge Musik* upward-firing cannon were widely used, enabling the night fighters to attack from beneath the bombers' undefended bellies. The German pilot had to be very careful to aim at the wing fuel tanks for there were occasions when, hit in the bomb bay, the bomber blew up with such violence that the night fighter was also destroyed. It was these massive mid-air explosions that gave rise to the RAF's belief that the Luftwaffe was employing some sort of 'scarecrow'–somehow causing huge explosions inside the bomber stream to demoralise the British crews! No such pyrotechnics were ever employed and, as previously remarked, the RAF remained wholly unaware of the existence of *Schräge Musik*.

For all the RAF's confidence that it was capable of bombing Germany into submission, the great night raids that constituted the Battle of Berlin during the winter of 1943-44 dispelled any British doubts that the Luftwaffe possessed the men, machines and means to destroy Bomber Command. The losses being inflicted certainly prevented the build-up of the Command to the point at which the War could be ended by bombing.

Individual German night fighter pilots frequently achieved big multiple scores against single raids, each bomber shot down taking with it a crew of seven men. Seven bombers were shot down by Heinz Prinz zu Sayn-Wittgenstein during one raid in July 1943; the great Heinz-Wolfgang Schnaufer despatched seven

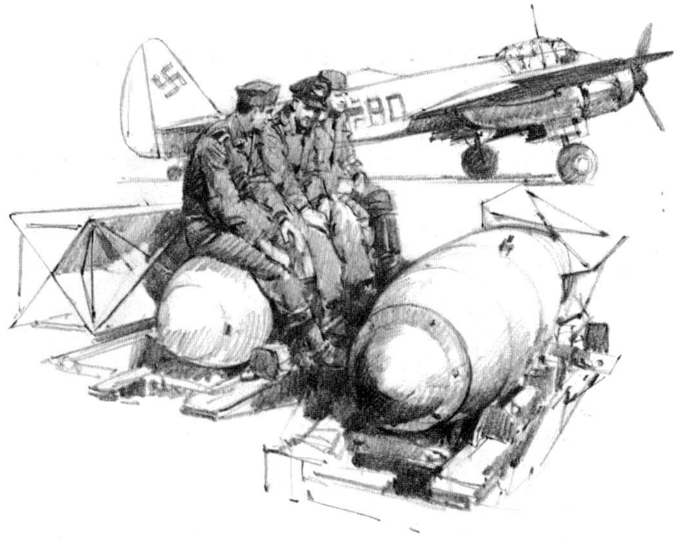

Following pages: *ground crews relax among their Ju 88s on the Eastern Front. Summer weather in Russia would have enabled the Luftwaffe to mount widespread bombing operations but for its constant shortage of fuel*

MICHAEL TURNER '85

Lancasters in 17 minutes on February 21, 1945; and Major Wilhelm Herget of *I./NJG 4* shot down eight on December 20, 1943. These were all eclipsed by the exploits of Hauptmann Martin Becker who, flying Ju 88s with *NJG 4* and *NJG 6* destroyed six heavy bombers on March 23, 1944, seven on the 31st of the same month (during the RAF's disastrous raid on Nuremburg when more than 100 bombers were lost), and no fewer than nine on March 14, 1945.

Just as a Junkers Ju 88 bomber had been the first German aircraft to fall on British soil on October 16, 1939, it was a Ju 88G intruder of *13./NJG 3* that was the last to fall, crashing in Yorkshire on March 5, 1945.

Germany's Flying Jeep – Fieseler Fi 156 Storch

In some respects the Fieseler Fi 156 *Storch* (Stork) was many years ahead of its time and was certainly unique in its class of light communications aircraft throughout the War, proving greatly superior to the Allied Taylorcrafts, Aeroncas and Stinsons. Indeed many an RAF and Army commander contrived to beg, borrow or steal a captured Storch for his own personal enjoyment! By the end of the War more than 40 such aircraft were in everyday use in Allied colours. . .

Designed to an RLM requirement issued in 1935 for an aircraft for army co-operation, gunner observation, communications and casualty evacuation, the Fieseler Fi 156 had to meet stringent demands for superlative low speed handling, very short take-off and landing characteristics, ease and speed of production and repair, and low cost. Beating several other competitors including a Focke-Wulf autogiro (the Fw 186), the Storch entered production in 1937 and quickly established itself as a firm favourite among Luftwaffe pilots. In common with so many other pre-War German aircraft a small number of Storchs was sent to Spain, where a *Kette* operated from El Burgo de Osma for a short time before being 'divvied up' among the German unit commanders for general liaison and communications work. On many occasions the use of the full-span flaps and leading edge slats enabled the aircraft to manoeuvre into very restricted spaces where the long-travel undercarriage allowed landings on stone-strewn surfaces. Indeed, in a 15-knot headwind the Storch required only 20 yards' landing run; its minimum flying speed was less than 30 mph, its top speed about 105 mph. Its bulged, extensively glazed cockpit canopy–which permitted the occupants to see almost vertically below the aircraft and gave an uninterrupted all-round view–gave rise to one of its widely-used nicknames, *Glaskasten* (or 'glass-box').

Most Fi 156As were distributed among Wehrmacht Divisional Staffs (the folding wings allowing the aircraft to be parked in motor transport parks with a reduced risk of damage), but others were used by senior *Luftgau* staffs until in 1939 a new version, the Fi 156C, was introduced. This featured a raised rear section of the cabin roof incorporating a mounting for a single 7.9-mm machine gun. A number of sub-variants was produced, the C-1 being a staff aircraft

With its ultra-short field performance the Fieseler Storch was the ideal light aircraft to provide a despatch service to front line units; depicted here is the long-range Fi 156C-5

with a just-perceptible improvement in comfort for its occupants, the C-2 was equipped for short-range battlefield surveillance, the C-3 was a multi-rôle version with wheel landing gear that could be changed for a pair of skis and powered by an improved Argus engine, while the C-5 was fitted with an extra, external fuel tank under the fuselage which almost trebled the aircraft's range to over 600 miles. Tropicalized versions, the C-3/Trop and C-5/Trop were also produced with a conical sand filter over the carburettor intake below the engine.

During the first two years of the War the Storch was not assigned operational duties with established units, a large number of aircraft being used *ad hoc* to evacuate wounded aircrew from operational airfields in France and the Low Countries during the Battle of Britain, although the C-series aircraft were not capable of accommodating stretcher cases. The first dedicated ambulance version (the D-1 *Sanitatsflugzeug*), appeared in 1941, being widely used on the Eastern Front and in the Mediterranean theatre (the later being the D-1/Trop). General Staff officers, particularly such well know figures as Albert Kesselring and Erwin Rommel, are said to have infinitely preferred to use their personal Storch rather than their larger, more prestigious aircraft, as the unheralded visit to front line units by the smaller aircraft lent welcome informality to their travels. No fewer than 15 aircraft were assigned to HQ, *X.Fliegerkorps* in Sicily in 1942.

Some of the longest-serving aeroplanes were those of the two *Wüstennotstaffeln* (desert rescue squadrons), the Storch being afforded priority care and maintenance, so prized were they among the operational aircrew! They continued to operate in Sicily in 1943, frequently weaving among the mountains to escape the attention of Allied fighters, to land beside some crashed aircraft to recover its crew and return it to its unit.

In Russia the Storch served operationally with *Heeresaufklärungsgruppen 14* and *21*, being used with ski landing gear during the first two harsh winters of the campaign. It was also used to deliver small groups of saboteurs behind the Russian lines with *Luftlande-geschwader 1* (LLG 1).

One of the final wartime flights by a Storch was made when Adolf Hitler ordered the distinguished woman pilot, Hanna Reitsch, to fly General Oberst Robert Ritter von Greim from Gatow into the centre of Berlin on April 26, 1945, for his formal promotion to command the Luftwaffe after the demise of Hermann Göring.

Condors Over the Atlantic – Focke-Wulf Fw 200

Wearing the famous 'world in a ring' markings of I.Gruppe, Kampfgeschwader 40, *a Focke-Wulf Fw 200C-3 Condor circles a burning tanker in the Atlantic during 1941*

Referred to by Winston Churchill as the 'Scourge of the Atlantic' the big four-engine Focke-Wulf Fw 200 Condor was hurriedly developed for long-range maritime duties from the famous pre-War Lufthansa airliner which had aroused considerable interest on account of a number of outstanding long-distance flights. Indeed at the outbreak of war only two Condors were held by the Luftwaffe – both transports, one of which was Hitler's official *Führermaschine*. Some of the Lufthansa airliners were taken over by the Luftwaffe at the time of the Norwegian campaign for use as transports by *KGrzbV 105*.

It was not however so much the fact that the Luftwaffe had not foreseen the need for a long-range maritime reconnaissance aircraft but that the one aircraft, the He 177, which was being developed for this rôle, was so far behind schedule that it would not enter service until 1942. The only aircraft therefore which promised reasonable adaptability in the short term was the Fw 200 and, bearing in mind the emphasis on the 'short term' the Fw 200 did a remarkably good job. Modification for its use in the maritime rôle owed a certain amount to work already done in response to a pre-War enquiry by Japan for such an aircraft (although in fact none was delivered), so that the first makeshift pre-production service aircraft (Fw 200C-0s) were delivered to the newly-formed *Kampfgeschwader 40* in Denmark before the end of the Norwegian campaign.

The first fully-militarised Condors, the Fw 200C-1

with long ventral gondola, a defensive armament of three machine guns and a 20-mm cannon, and a bomb load of up to four 550-lb bombs, joined *KG 40* in June 1940 and, flying from Bordeaux-Merignac, started operations against Britain; apart from laying mines outside ports their principal task was to fly long patrols in the Western Approaches to report on the approach of deep water convoys. One of the much publicised achievements of *KG 40* was the attack by Oberleutnant Bernhard Jope on the 42,000-ton liner *Empress of Britain* off the north coast of Ireland on October 26, 1940 which left the big ship crippled; she was then torpedoed and sunk by a U-boat. Jope was awarded the Knight's Cross (he later commanded *KG 40*, and received the Oakleaves as a Major).

KG 40's operations after the Battle of Britain contributed to the U-boats' fast-increasing toll of British shipping as improved versions of the Condor, with heavier armament, search radar and improved bombsight, entered service. Often operating far out over the Atlantic the big aircraft searched for convoys and, having found them, followed and radioed the ships' position, course and speed. The German Navy in turn would order any conveniently stationed U-boats to the attack. Occasionally the Condors would themselves attack the ships in an effort to slow the convoys, but when the British started employing Hurricane fighters the Luftwaffe pilots reverted to their shadowing rôle.

Then, at the end of 1941, the Royal Navy began operating escort carriers whose fighters took an increasing toll of the Condors; *KG 40* began to disperse, its *I.Gruppe* being transferred to Norway in 1942 for operations against the North Cape convoys. When these convoys also introduced the escort carrier *KG 40* was split up further at the beginning of 1943 as two Staffeln were ordered to start flying supplies into the Stalingrad pockets as *KGrzbV 200* under Major Hans-Jürgen Villiers. Losses from all causes continued to limit the number of Condors available for operations, the aircraft simply not being adequately robust for operational load carrying and manoeuvres; more than 20 aircraft were to be lost as the result of wing spar failures and collapse of the centre fuselage structure. Such loss was not insignificant in a total production of about 250 aircraft.

In 1943 *KG 40* recovered two of its Gruppen to France for a new phase of attacks on convoys, particularly those sailing from Gibraltar to Britain. Acting on reports from German agents in Spain of the sailing of the convoys, the very long range Junkers Ju 290s of *Fernaufklärungsgruppe 5* would locate and shadow the ships. An attack would then be launched by a minimum of four Condors of *III./KG 40*, the Fw 200C-4 now being equipped with the efficient *Hohentwiel* search radar. However, as the crews were under orders by *Fliegerführer Atlantik* not to attack the convoys from below 10,000 ft, so as to avoid losses from the ships' guns, scarcely any worthwhile results were achieved.

Before the end of 1943 *KG 40* started receiving Germany's new anti-shipping missile, the rocket-propelled radio-controlled Henschel Hs 293, the new Fw 200C-8 being intended to carry a pair of them under the wings. But on the first operational sortie with them the Condor ran in with an RAF Sunderland flying boat and was shot down. The Geschwader persevered with the Hs 293 but still failed to come up with any success and, following the loss of its airfields in Western France after the Normandy landings, the few surviving Condors were withdrawn to Germany where they once more assumed the transport rôle.

Kurt Tank's Butcher Bird – Focke-Wulf Fw 190

When RAF pilots first reported encountering the Focke-Wulf Fw 190 fighters over the English Channel in 1941 their estimates of the German aircraft's performance were largely discounted by their Intelligence Officers who simply could not countenance an aircraft with a big bulky radial engine outperforming the sleek British Spitfire V, even if their earlier suspicions that the Luftwaffe was using captured American Curtiss Hawk 75s were no longer being voiced. As Spitfire losses began to increase, the RAF was forced to accept that the Germans had indeed succeeded in producing a new and deadly fighter.

In 1937, when the Messerschmitt Bf 109 was first entering service, the RLM issued a requirement for a

Use of the Focke-Wulf Fw 190A-3/U1 fighter-bomber of the JG 2 *and* JG 26 Jabo Staffeln *over the Dieppe beaches in August 1942 came as an unpleasant surprise to the Allies*

109 replacement (at almost exactly the same time that the British Air Ministry was calling for a successor to the Hurricane, which emerged as the Hawker Typhoon). First flown on June 1, 1939 by Flugkapitän Hans Sander, the Fw 190 originally featured a large ducted spinner, soon to be discarded owing to engine overheating, and appeared in production form early in 1941 as an extremely attractive, compact aeroplane with an exceptionally clean installation of the 14 cylinder 1,660-hp BMW 801 radial engine. Unlike the Bf 109, the new Fw 190 had a very wide track landing gear which retracted inwards, considerably improving the landing characteristics. With a speed of around 410 mph the Fw 190A-1 was armed with four 7.9-mm machine guns, but this light armament was acknowledged as being only temporary.

The first Fw 190A-1s served with *6.Staffel, Jagdgeschwader 26* <*Schlageter*> under Oberleutnant Karl Borris at Le Bourget in August 1941, having their first brush with Spitfires the following month and quickly acquiring the unofficial name *Würger* ('Butcher Bird'). By the beginning of the following year the whole of Galland's *II./JG 26* (led by Hauptmann Joachim Müncheberg) and *III./JG 26* (Oberleutnant Josef 'Pips' Priller) had been re-equipped and, despite their relatively small numbers, were quickly establishing their superiority over the Spitfire V, which RAF Fighter Command had selected to become its standard fighter for offensive operations over the Channel following the Battle of Britain. *JG 26's* first major operation arrived when, under Galland's command, the German fighter force in France was ordered to cover the escape back to Germany of the *Scharnhorst, Gneisenau* and *Prinz Eugen* from Brest on February 12, 1942. The Fw 190s of *III./JG 26* decimated the Swordfish torpedo biplanes led by Lieut-Cdr Eugene Esmonde VC DSO in their legendary attack on the warships. The Luftwaffe's victory proved somewhat hollow on that occasion as Fighter Command scarcely reacted until the German ships were already sailing out of range of its bases.

The following month the Fw 190A-3 appeared in service with an armament of four 20-mm cannon and, as production increased rapidly, this version re-equipped *II./JG 26* and the whole of Oberst Walter Oesau's *JG 2*, the only other fighter Wing still based in France. On June 23 the RAF got its hands on an intact example when a *III./JG 2* pilot, Oberleutnant Armin

Faber, landed his A-3 at Pembrey in South Wales following a navigational error. The German machine was quickly evaluated by British pilots and information on its various strengths and weaknesses passed on to the operational squadrons.

Thus by the date of the famous British landings at Dieppe on August 19 that year the RAF felt it had the measure of the Fw 190. It was also hoped to engage the new German fighter with the RAF's own new fighters, the Typhoon and Spitfire IX, the latter hurriedly introduced specifically to counter the Fw 190.

The RAF mounted a huge umbrella of Spitfire V squadrons over the Dieppe landing, the majority of them patrolling between 10,000 and 20,000 ft. Unfortunately what was not known was that a new fighter-bomber version of the Fw 190A-3, the A-3/U1, had been introduced, capable of carrying a single 1,100-lb bomb. A number of these streaked in over the beaches at low level, hitting two ships before making good their escape. High above, *JG 2* and *JG 26* refrained from engaging the Spitfire squadrons until it was discovered how long each could remain on patrol, but in mid-morning attacks developed as some of the Spitfires were ending their patrol period, the British fighters being caught at a disadvantage owing to their shortage of fuel. Even the Spitfire IX and Typhoon squadrons were unable to engage the Fw 190s as they were held too far from the landing area (and two Typhoons were accidentally shot down by the Canadian-flown Spitfire IXs). The result of the day's battles was considerable disappointment for the British, fewer than 50 German aircraft being shot down (scarcely any Fw 190s), while the RAF lost 106, of which 97 were destroyed by the Fw 190s. The new fighter had recovered the initiative over the English Channel, and the Luftwaffe was quick to exploit it.

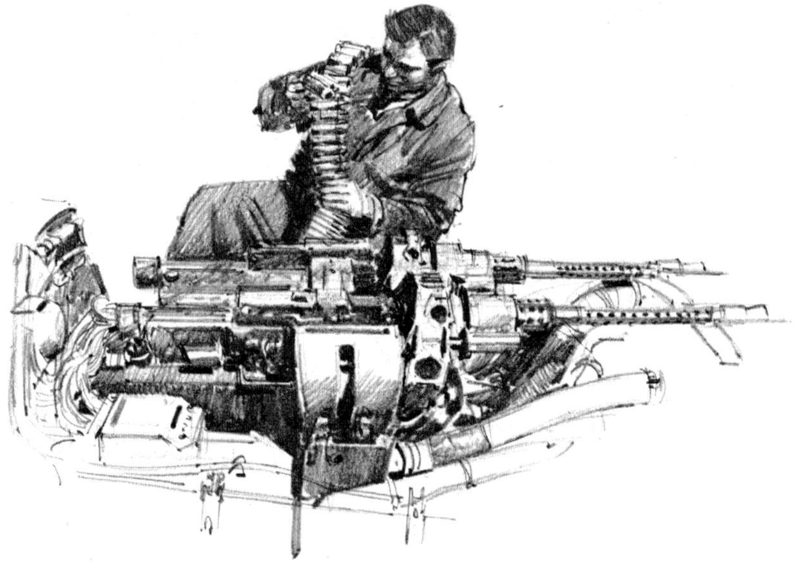

Wild Boars – Focke-Wulf Fw 190A-5

It has remained something of a mystery to this day why the Luftwaffe delayed introducing the Fw 190 into service on the Russian Front until the late summer of 1942, almost exactly one year after equipping *6./JG 26* in France. Indeed the Fw 190A-4 with water-methanol power-boosting and the A-5, similar but with a slightly longer nose, were issued to units in France and the Mediterranean in greater numbers during 1942 and early 1943 than to units in the East.

Following the *débâcle* over Dieppe the Luftwaffe embarked on a series of tip-and-run raids on English towns and cities in the Southern Counties, including London. Although probably no more than 60 Fw 190A-3s and A-4s were ever available these raids by the '*Jabos*' (*Jagdbomberstaffeln*) caused the RAF to redeploy more than a dozen squadrons for low level defence. Outstanding among these sneak raids were an attack on Canterbury on October 31, 1942, on London in January 1943, and Ashford, Eastbourne and Hastings in March. On April 14 the Focke-Wulfs destroyed a ball-bearing factory in Chelmsford, Essex. In many instances Typhoons (and ultimately special low altitude Spitfire XIIs) were positioned on their runways ready to take off at a moment's notice, but still failed to take a significant toll of the raiders, most of the 33 Fw 190s shot down in these attacks falling to

The Luftwaffe managed to deploy a number of Fw 190 fighter-bombers against the Allies during the invasion of Sicily; here, with hurried attempts at camouflage, a SKG 10 aircraft undergoes field maintenance

the Bofors guns. The unit involved in these attacks was *Schnellkampfgeschwader 10* (Fast Bomber Wing 10) formed out of the *Jabo Staffeln* of *JG 2* and *JG 26*, but, like so many specialist units, *SKG 10* was split up and distributed among other fronts, only *I.Gruppe* remaining in France. *II.*, *III.* and *IV.* were heavily involved in action against the Allied invasion of Sicily and suffered considerable losses from the huge number of Spitfires which kept up incessant attacks on the Axis airfields.

The Luftwaffe was now faced with Allied pressure in the East, South and over the Reich itself, and still the OKL would not sanction all-out production of fighters. Adolf Galland has recorded his opinion that had priority been afforded to the production of Fw 190s in the late summer of 1943–instead of squandering some 60 per cent of German industrial effort on other aircraft that could no longer influence the outcome of the War–Germany's production of this excellent aircraft could have matched Allied fighter production by the end of the year. The nation still possessed large numbers of excellent pilots at that time and the Allies still had not made any serious efforts to attack the German oil industry.

Thus when the USAAF stepped up its daylight attacks in mid-1943 the Luftwaffe possessed 22 *Jagdgruppen* equipped with Fw 190A-4s and A-5s, a total of around 450 aircraft; by the end of August, following the big American raids on Regensburg and Schweinfurt (when 60 heavy bombers were destroyed and 100 damaged), the *Befehlshaber Mitte*, Central Area Command, fielded six such Gruppen, withdrawn from the Eastern Front and Italy for home defence.

Both the night fighter *Geschwader*, *NJG 1* and *NJG 2*, were conducting trials with Fw 190s as night fighters, but it was in another aspect that the use of single-seaters at night that was to spotlight the growing crisis in the supply of fighters. Following the RAF's use of 'Window' in the Battle of Hamburg, a 'device' that had rendered the conventional radar-controlled night fighters virtually helpless, Major Hajo Herrmann of the Luftwaffe's Operational Staff, recommended the formation of a Wing of single-seat fighters to operate at night. These were to attack British bombers silhouetted against fires on the ground, illuminated by searchlights or, whenever possible, in moonlight, and above all thus be wholly independent of radar and unaffected by its jamming. Given the codename *Wilde Sau*, these tactics were employed by the first such Wing, *Jagdgeschwader 300* under the command of Herrmann himself and, after some setbacks, they began to pay handsome dividends. Based at Bonn/Hangelar, Oldenburg and Rheine, the three *Gruppen* of *JG 300*, flying Focke-Wulf Fw 190A-5s and Bf 109Gs, shot down more than 150 British bombers in August and September. Herrmann became a national hero and was given command of *Jagddivision 30*, ultimately comprising *JG 300*, now led by Oberstleutnant Kurt Kettner, *JG 301* by Major Helmut Weinrich and *JG 302* by Major Janssen.

In the early stages of the winter Battle of Berlin the *Wilde Sau* (Wild Boar) fighters continued to shoot down British bombers in large numbers. However, because of the shortage of fighters, it was necessary to hold a high proportion of them available for daytime combat against the American raids, with the result that wear and tear, and hurried maintenance took a heavy toll of aircraft; fatigue among the pilots who were often forced to fly in bad weather at night brought about an increasing spate of accidents, so that by early 1944 there were seldom more than 20–30 aircraft serviceable for combat on any particular night–from a force of almost 200 fighters. Nevertheless, such were the problems created by RAF jamming, the *Wilde Sau* Wings continued to operate, though on a diminishing scale, for the remainder of the War.

Defence of the Reich – Focke-Wulf Fw 190A-8

When eventually Focke-Wulf Fw 190A-4s reached the Eastern Front they quickly became extremely popular among the fighter pilots, partly on account of their air-cooled engines and wide-track landing gear which made operation from the poorly-surfaced Russian airfields much simpler than with the Gustav. Successive versions and sub-variants followed in 1943 which introduced progressively heavier armament. To facilitate adaptation to mount special weapons for particular missions a wide range of *Rustsatz* (modification kits) was introduced. Early in 1944 the Fw 190A-8 appeared with nitrous oxide power-boosting which enabled a heavily-laden aircraft to make a short high speed dash if attacked by another fighter. A fully-equipped A-8 might well carry a 1,100-lb bomb under the fuselage, an internal armament of four 20-mm cannon and two 30-mm guns in external packs under the wings. Some aircraft were fitted with ski undercarriage for operations during the Russian winter of 1944.

By then however the Soviet Air Force possessed large numbers of excellent fighters, including the Lavochkin La-5 which not only resembled the Fw 190 but also possessed a similar performance. This, and the creation of the so-called 'Assault Wings' resulted in the Focke-Wulf being used almost exclusively for ground attack on the Eastern Front under protection afforded by Gustavs. However in those rare instances wherein the Junkers Ju 87G was retained for ground attack, such as on Rudel's *III./St.G 2*, the cover was afforded by the Fw 190, in this case by *I./JG 51* <*Mölders*> under Major Erich Leie. This pilot was typical of the long-serving German officer who remained on operations for almost five years without a break, flying Emils during the Battle of Britain with *JG 2*, then Fw 190s during 1942-43 with *JG 51* before taking command of *JG 77* and once more flying Bf 109s in 1945. Awarded the Knight's Cross and nominated for the Oakleaves he was killed attempting to bale out after colliding with a Russian fighter on March 7, 1945

A 'Dora-Nine', sporting Defence of the Reich fuselage bands, in action against US Eighth Air Force B-24J Liberators of the 489th Bomb Group in the daylight air battles over Germany

MICHAEL TURNER

when his score stood at 118 victories (of which 43 were scored against the RAF).

A somewhat macabre chapter in the history of the Fw 190 opened late in 1943 when Göring personally ordered the formation of the Fw 190-equipped *Stürmstaffel 1*. Staffed both by volunteers and pilots who had committed some breach of discipline, this Staffel initially flew specially armoured Fw 190A-6s, each pilot ordered to attack enemy bomber formations and being required to sign a declaration that he would destroy at least one bomber if necessary, as a last resort, by ramming as a token of atonement. Failure would be regarded as cowardice and treated accordingly. Limited success attended *Stürmstaffel 1* but, after losing almost all its pilots and aircraft, the first of several new units *IV.(Stürm)/JG 3 <Udet>*, was formed as a regular line Gruppe under Major Wilhelm Moritz in March 1944, flying Fw 190A-8s. Although carrying even more armour than the A-6s, the A-8/R7s seldom rammed the American bombers, being able to withstand the bombers' machine gun armament as they closed to short range to blast away with their own heavy armament. In one memorable attack on July 7, 1944 *IV.(Stürm)/JG* shot down 32 American heavy bombers for the loss of only two Fw 190s.

While Moritz had to be taken off operations due to complete battle exhaustion in November, other *Stürmgruppen* had been created. Their tactics were almost exclusively confined to the close-in pass using the 21-cm WGr rocket. Despite frequent instances when American P-51 pilots were able to dogfight with the Fw 190s, their 0.50-in machine guns could do little against the heavily armoured German fighters. Not surprisingly *Stürmjäger* Gruppen were created for use of *Wilde Sau* tactics at night, *II.* and *IV. (Stürm)/JG 300* flying 30-mm gun-armed Fw 190A-8/R2s.

Fw 190A-8s equipped the only Wing, *JG 26*, that was combat-deployed in Northern France when the Allies landed in Normandy on June 6, 1944. However only two aircraft got airborne, flown by the *Geschwaderkommodore*, Oberst 'Pip' Priller and his wingman, in the early hours of the invasion. In an effort to mount some opposition to the vast armadas of Allied aircraft the Luftwaffe rushed fighter units to France from other hard-pressed fronts and within a fortnight more than 14 Fw 190 Gruppen with A-5s, -6s, -7s and -8s were trying to stem the tide of British and American aircraft over the invasion area; among these were two *Stürmgruppen* of *JG 3* and *JG 300*. Nevertheless, although the Allied fighter pilots found the ground attack Fw 190s extremely difficult to shoot down as the Luftwaffe pilots invariably used their power-boosting to escape from harm, the massed Bofors guns shot down large numbers and, one by one, the *Jagdgeschwader* were disbanded or withdrawn to Germany to re-equip.

The best Fw 190 version was the 'long-nose' D-Series with in-line Jumo 213 engine installed in an annular cowling, of which the 'Dora-Nine' (D-9) saw most service, starting in the autumn of 1944 with *III./JG 54 <Grünherz>* under Major Robert 'Bazi' Weiss. Initially given the task of defending the experimental jet fighter bases from Allied attacks, Dora-Nines quickly re-equipped a number of 'Defence of the Reich' *Gruppen* and were widely considered to be Germany's best piston-engine interceptors, capable of dogfighting the best Allied fighters as well as knocking down American bombers with their heavy cannon armament.

Well over 200 Fw 190s were involved in the final great air attack (Operation *Bodenplatte*) of New Year's Day 1945 but, as with the other aircraft taking part, the 190s suffered appalling wastage and, far worse, irreplaceable pilots never returned. Yet, even in the final chaotic month of the War, German factories were still capable of turning out more than 800 of Kurt Tank's remarkable fighter.

The Tank Buster – Henschel Hs 129

The Henschel Hs 129 twin-engine ground attack aircraft was unique among Axis and Allied aircraft in being conceived to perform a combat rôle without the Service being able to define accurately either the performance or armament requirements with any confidence. One is left with a distinct impression that the RLM in 1937 simply invited Henschel and Focke-Wulf to produce prototypes capable of mounting a pair of 20-mm cannon and powered by two small 465-hp Argus engines, and then see what they could do. The Focke-Wulf tender was the Fw 189C, a version of the light twin-engine twin-boom reconnaissance aircraft, but this proved very unpopular when evaluated by the Luftwaffe, and in any case the prototype crashed during tests. The under-powered Hs 129, with its cramped armoured box of a cockpit, was also severely criticised; indeed so constricted was the Hs 129's cockpit that some instruments had to be fitted on the sides of the engine nacelles! A few Argus-powered examples were delivered for evaluation by *Lehrgeschwader 2* in 1940, but this only stiffened the Luftwaffe's resolve to have nothing to do with the aircraft as it stood.

Friedrich Nicolaus, Henschel's Chief Designer, accordingly undertook a complete revision of the aircraft, employing captured French Gnome-Rhône 14M radials which produced 700 hp. Deliveries of this version, the Hs 129B of which 858 were eventually produced, started at the end of 1942. It certainly proved less unpopular than the earlier, desperately underpowered and sluggish aeroplane, although the heavily-framed cockpit canopy with armoured glass panels up to 3-in thick severely restricted the pilot's field of view. Not surprisingly the Luftwaffe immediately began demanding greater armament, the most widely-used variant being the 129B-1/R2 with two 20-mm and two 7.9-mm guns on the sides of the fuselage, a single 30-mm cannon below the nose and two packs each containing 48 2-kg anti-personnel fragmentation bombs.

When however the first Hs 129Bs were delivered to the new *Schlachtgeschwader 1* in mid-1942 it was soon discovered that the French engines were most unreliable, being prone to seizing in dusty conditions and being unable to contend with the slightest battle damage. Nevertheless the growing weight of armour being thrown against German forces in Russia and North Africa obliged the Luftwaffe to introduce an anti-tank aircraft quickly, so that *4./Sch.G 1* was despatched post-haste to the Eastern Front in May, and a second unit, *4./Sch.G 2* to North Africa in November.

The latter, its strength reduced to only eight aircraft even before it arrived in Libya, attempted to bring the Hs 129 into action but with little success; following the failure to produce an efficient sand filter, the pervading dust and not the Allies finally defeated *4./Sch.G 2*. Another unit, *8./Sch.G 2*, had better fortune in Tunisia but after February 1943 engine failures and forced landings caused the survivors to be withdrawn to Sardinia.

It was on the Eastern Front that the Hs 129 gave its best service, puny though it was in all conscience, bearing in mind the great hordes of Soviet tanks that were now being thrown against the Wehrmacht. By mid-1943 eight Staffeln of Hs 129s, with a total of 82 aircraft, were serving on the Front, of which *4.* and *8./Sch.G 1* and *4.* and *8./Sch.G 2* were based on the Central Sector at Mikoyanovka with 60 aircraft in readiness for the enormous armoured battle that was clearly about to develop as German forces prepared to mount a great pincer movement at Kursk. At the height of the battle Hauptmann Bruno Meyer, a veteran of the Polish and French campaigns, the Battle of Britain, the Balkans and Tunisian campaign and now commanding the four Hs 129 Staffeln, spotted a dangerous thrust by Soviet tanks towards the flank of the *II.SS Panzerkorps* near Belgorod. Calling up his four Staffeln in turn for a series of attacks, Meyer and his pilots halted the thrust, setting about 20 tanks on fire and forcing the remainder to retreat.

Hs 129s certainly accounted for a sizeable proportion of the 1,100 Russian tanks claimed destroyed by the Luftwaffe at Kursk, their success prompting the grouping of all these aircraft into a newly-formed *IV.(Panzer)/Schlachtgeschwader 9* which, under the command of Bruno Meyer (now a Major), was given a roving commission to undertake anti-tank operations throughout the length of the Eastern Front.

The 30-mm cannon proved incapable of penetrating the frontal armour of Soviet tanks being

Following pages: *Although the Henschel Hs 129 scored a number of successes against Russian tanks (of which the T-34 was the most formidable) at the battle of Kursk, the Luftwaffe was by then too weak to seriously influence events*

MICHAEL TURNER '85

introduced in 1943 and the Hs 129B-2/R4 was developed to mount the huge 75-mm gun under the fuselage; this gun was about 20 ft long and its barrel recoiled some 3 ft when fired!

Despite its general unpopularity the Hs 129 was developed to mount even less orthodox weapons in the Germans' desperate efforts to stem the Russian advance. Eleven-inch WGr 28 rockets, the Gero flame-thrower and the extraordinary SG 113A rocket mortar were all flown; the latter comprised six mortars each firing a single 77-mm missile vertically downwards as the aircraft passed over an enemy tank, triggered by a photo-electric cell.

The Luftwaffe's Heavy Brigade – Junkers Ju 290 (and other very large aircraft)

After the plans to create a German strategic bomber force were abandoned in 1936 the two aircraft projects associated with it, the Dornier Do 19 and the Junkers Ju 89, were also officially discontinued. The latter however was used as a basis for a transport, the Ju 90, an impressive and attractive aeroplane which first flew on August 28, 1937 but which crashed the following year. Subsequently a total of 14 of these big 40-passenger aircraft was built, being intended for Lufthansa; the survivors were impressed into Luftwaffe service, some employed as transports during the Norwegian campaign. Seven served on the *Viermotorige*

Among the aircraft pressed into service to support the German Army trapped at Stalingrad were some Ju 290s, but as the Russians tightened their grip the big aircraft were deprived of suitable landing strips

MICHAEL TURNER '85

Transportstaffel (four-engine transport squadron) for delivery of supplies to Stalingrad in January 1943.

One of the Ju 90s had however been withdrawn in 1939 and returned to Junkers for development into a transport more exactly tailored to Luftwaffe requirements. A larger wing with four BMW 801 radial engines was substituted in what was initially termed the Ju 90S but was soon re-numbered the Ju 290. When the production version, the Ju 290A-1, appeared in 1942 it featured a defensive armament of three 20-mm cannon and three 13-mm heavy machine guns. Two of these aircraft as well as the first prototype, joined the *Viermotorige Transportstaffel* for the Stalingrad supply missions (the latter aircraft being destroyed in an accident on January 14, 1943).

While the Ju 290A-1s continued to serve with transport units in the Mediterranean later in 1943 the basic aircraft was undergoing development as a maritime reconnaissance replacement for the Focke-Wulf Fw 200 Condor, and 37 such aircraft (Ju 290A-2s, -3s, -4s, -5s, and -7s) were completed, most of which served with the three *Staffeln* of *Fernaufklärungsgruppe 5* (*FAGr 5*, long-range reconnaissance Group 5). These aircraft, which differed principally in details of radar, were based at Mont de Marsan in Southwest France during the latter half of 1943 and worked in collaboration with *KG 40*, transmitting sighting reports of convoys for subsequent attack by the Condors and U-boats. The Ju 290A-7 was itself an attack version and was able to carry up to three Henschel Hs 293 rocket missiles for anti-shipping strikes. The single A-6 was a 50-seater developed for the personal use of Hitler; it was later used for clandestine operations with *KG 200* at Finsterwalde, and on April 25, 1945 was flown to Barcelona with a load of Nazi officials seeking to escape the clutches of the Allies.

Some of the Ju 290's most remarkable flights were those by three aircraft withdrawn from *FAGr 5* and modified to carry more than 5,000 gallons of fuel. These aircraft made a number of non-stop flights from Odessa to Japanese air bases in Manchuria, delivering cargoes of such war supplies as six Jumo 004 jet engines and various radar components to Germany's Far Eastern ally; on their return flight they brought useful war commodities such as rubber latex and exotic metals. At the end of the War the Ju 290E was being developed as a heavy bomber capable of carrying over 40,000 lb of bombs – roughly double the load of a B-29 Superfortress. The wheel had turned full circle. . .

* * *

A number of other very large German aircraft were produced during the War, including those conceived in the '*Amerika-Bomber*' programme, although at conception in 1940 the likelihood of America entering the War against Germany seemed remote. The idea of an aircraft flying from Europe to the United States with a bomb load, and returning, was certainly intriguing and two aircraft, the Messerschmitt Me 264 and the Junkers Ju 390, came to be built. The former, a new design but using four Ju 88-type engine installations to speed development, was the first to fly, in December 1942, one year after the United States had entered the War. With a span almost exactly the same as that of the B-29 Superfortress, there is no doubt but that the aircraft could have reached America and return (it had a maximum endurance of more than 40 hours), but interest waned and the prototype found its way on to the Luftwaffe's large transport unit, *Transportstaffel 5*.

Rather more interest was envinced in the Junkers Ju 390, indeed a very large aircraft powered by six 1,700-hp BMW 801 radial engines, being an enlarged development of the Ju 290. Two prototypes were completed and flown in the second half of 1943, the second example carrying *Hohentwiel* search radar and a defensive armament of five 20-mm cannon and three 13-mm heavy machine guns. This aircraft underwent operational evaluation by *Fernaufklärungsgruppe 5* at Mont de Marsan the following year and during the course of its trials flew to within 12 miles of New York before returning safely to base!

The Hornet – Messerschmitt Me 410 Hornisse

Long before the Messerschmitt Bf 110 gave cause for concern with its failure to match contemporary interceptor fighters, the normal process to acquire a replacement had begun in 1937. Probably reflecting Göring's infatuation with the *Zerstörer* concept, no fewer than one thousand Messerschmitt Me 210s were ordered off the drawing board by the RLM. This turned out to be a supremely arrogant and ill-advised step.

The first prototype Me 210, which superficially resembled the Bf 110 with twin fins and rudders, flew on September 2, 1939 and from the outset had very bad directional stability. A large single fin and rudder was substituted which marginally improved the handling but, even so, the second prototype crashed one year later.

By that time operational problems were surfacing with the Bf 110, and steps were taken to rush the Me 210 into service. It was primarily for this purpose that Rubensdörffer's *Erprobungsgruppe 210* had been formed at the beginning of the Battle of Britain; when it became obvious that the Me 210's entry into service was *not* imminent the task of *Erpr.Gr. 210* shifted to that of operational pathfinding.

The Me 210 nevertheless was rushed into service as a fighter-bomber in 1941 with *II./ZG 1* on the Eastern Front but an unchecked spate of fatal accidents (caused by spins from which the aircraft displayed a reluctance to recover) brought about a halt to production in April 1942, resulting in an enormous financial loss by Messerschmitt.

Although Me 210s continued in service, and some were even used in raids on the British Isles late in 1942, Messerschmitt was engaged in trying to salvage something from the wreckage of the *Zerstörer* idea, and came up with the Me 410 *Hornisse* (Hornet). Scarcely distinguishable externally from the ill-starred 210, the new fighter-bomber was powered by 1,750-hp DB 603A engines in lengthened nacelles, and incorporated all the modifications and remedies that had been devised for its predecessor. The result, perhaps surprisingly, was an excellent aeroplane and one the Luftwaffe was quick to appreciate.

Me 410As were first delivered to front line units in May 1943, A-1 fighter-bombers going to *5./KG 2* for night attacks on the British Isles, A-1/U1 reconnaissance aircraft to *2.Staffel, Fernaufklärungsgruppe 122* at Trapani, and A-1/U2 bomber-destroyers to

III.Gruppe, Zerstörergeschwader 1 at Gerbini, both in Sicily.

The two latter units were not fully worked up with their new aircraft when the Allies landed in Sicily and they suffered severely before the guns of the Spitfire and P-38 pilots. Over Britain however the Me 410A night bomber proved formidable, carrying either a pair of 2,200-lb or eight 110-lb bombs and possessing a top speed of almost 390 mph. Their speed of approach to their targets frequently defeated the somewhat ponderous raid reporting procedures of the Royal Observer Corps, while only the best of the Mosquito night fighter crews seemed able to cope with the low flying raiders. *5./KG 2's* first loss was suffered on July 13, 1943 when a 410 fell to the guns of a Mosquito; a similar aircraft fell to the guns of Wing Commander John Cunningham, CO of No 85 Squadron at West Malling, on January 2, 1944–the last aircraft to be shot down by the famous British night fighter pilot.

Another bomber unit to receive the *Hornisse* was *I./KG 51 <Edelweiss>*, commanded by Major Klaus Häberlen, which was withdrawn from the Russian Front to Germany in May 1943 and received Me 410A-1/U2s in place of its Ju 88 bombers in June (Häberlen was awarded the Knight's Cross in July for his outstanding service in Russia). Problems arose in converting to the new *Zerstörer*, for it had generally been thought that the Gruppe would continue in the night bombing rôle, but with the increasing American daylight raids it was as a bomber-destroyer unit that Häberlen's pilots found themselves being re-trained. Ironically Häberlen was replaced as *Kommandeur* by Major Wolf-Dietrich Meister on October 11, just three

An Me 410 Hornisse *of* V.Gruppe, Kampfgeschwader 2, *sweeps low over Brighton's Palace Pier in a snap dusk raid during the winter of 1943–44. Such attacks tested Britain's night defences to the full*

days before the big American raid on Schweinfurt, which *I./KG 51* was not called on to engage.

Evidently the Luftwaffe was already having second thoughts about using *Zerstörer* aircraft against the daylight raids (although Me 410s were to be used increasingly in this rôle in 1944), and *I./KG 51* was moved to Evreux in France in December and the following month started night operations against

England, the raids continuing until the end of May 1944. During this time the Me 410s attacked London, Brighton, Bristol, Portsmouth and Cambridge; it was in a raid on Cambridge on April 23 that Major Dietrich Puttfarken, *Staffelkapitän* of the *Gruppe's 1.Staffel* and a Knight's Cross holder, was shot down and killed. After the Normandy landings the Me 410s were switched to ground support operations but when about a dozen aircraft had been lost in six weeks the unit was withdrawn to Germany to re-equip with the Me 262 *Stürmvogel* jet bomber.

To Carry the Army's Heaviest Loads – Messerschmitt Me 323 Gigant

Design conventions were no obstacle to great ingenuity among German manufacturers during the Second World War, for they produced such extraordinary aircraft as the asymmetric Blohm und Voss Bv 141, the 'twinned' Heinkel He 111Z, the submarine-portable Arado Ar 231 and the huge Messerschmitt Me 323.

The latter, with a wing span of 180 ft, was in effect a powered version of the Messerschmitt Me 321 *Gigant* (Giant) glider which had first been towed into the air by a Junkers Ju 90 in March 1941. Originally conceived to support an invasion of Britain, the *Gigant* glider entered service with the *Grossraumlastensegler 321* (literally 'high capacity glider unit 321') at Leipheim only two months later, commanded by Fritz Morzik who was to win the Knight's Cross for his achievements at Demyansk less than a year later. Capable of carrying up to 120 fully-armed troops, 22 tons of supplies or an 88-mm dual-purpose gun, the *Gigant* remained in service for much of the remainder of the War, serving with *Grossraumlastensegler-Kommando 2 ((GS)Kdo 2)* at Regensburg and elsewhere. Its customary towing aircraft was to be the Junkers Ju 290, and ultimately the He 111Z *Zwilling*. On other occasions a trio of Bf 110 fighters (the '*Troika-Schlepp*') was used to haul the huge glider into the air. About 200 Me 321 gliders were produced.

Almost as the first *Gigant* glider was making its first flight a new project was being initiated to mount four of the French Gnome-Rhône 14 radial engines in the Me 321 to produce a 'conventional' transport aircraft–also to be known as the '*Gigant*'. However initial flight tests which started in April 1942 showed it to be badly underpowered, so the number of engines was simply increased to six, this expedient enabling the aircraft to take-off with something like its normal load of 130 troops; on occasions of emergency–such as

Following pages: *Me 323 transports were widely used behind the Eastern Front to deliver military equipment; when however they came within reach of Allied fighters the folly of using such aircraft was soon realised*

MICHAEL TURNER '85

Messerschmitt Me 321 glider gets airborne, towed by a Heinkel He 111Z and rocket assistance

evacuations of garrisons–more than 200 men were often crammed inside, recourse to the use of rockets being necessary to get the aircraft into the air. Once airborne the huge machine was almost entirely without directional stability and a pair of flight engineers were constantly engaged in juggling the six throttles to maintain a straight and level heading. Of course, with a normal cruising speed of around 120 mph, the Me 323 was appallingly vulnerable and therefore fairly bristled with defensive guns, with half a dozen 7.9-mm machine guns in the nose and upper fuselage and up to 10 infantry machine guns firing through ports in the fuselage sides. Later, as even these guns proved inadequate, a couple of 20-mm cannon in turrets were added above the fuselage, as well as gun positions in the upper surface of each wing between the outboard pairs of engines, each with a 13-mm heavy machine gun.

The Me 323 first entered service in November 1942 with *I./KGzbV 323* in the Mediterranean, at the time of the Torch landings and shortly after the Battle of El Alamein. Axis shipping losses were running at a high rate and so the nine Me 323D-1s were heavily occupied with ferrying fuel and other vital stores–usually at night–between Sicily and Tripolitania. In March 1943 the Geschwader's second Gruppe received the first Me 323D-6s with the increased defensive armament and within a fortnight the number of these aircraft on the air bridge to the Axis forces trapped in Tunisia had risen to about 40. Disaster struck on April 22 when seven squadrons of Spitfires and P-40 Kittyhawks descended on a formation of 27 Me 323s escorted by some Gustavs. No fewer than 21 of the huge transports, each loaded with about 15 tons of fuel desperately needed by the Afrika Korps, were shot down, the waters of the Sicilian Strait being dotted by great columns of oily black smoke to mark the graves of the victims.

On a number of other occasions, as the Germans pulled their garrisons out of the Mediterranean islands in 1943 and 1944 Me 323s, often greatly overloaded with soldiers, were caught and shot down by Allied fighters.

By 1944 however most surviving Me 323s were serving with *I.* and *II.Gruppen* of *Transportgeschwader 5* on the Russian Front; the most widely used version was the 323E-2 which, with more powerful engines could carry almost 30 tons of fuel or a military field command truck. Nevertheless, as it was forced to operate from very poorly surfaced airfields, it became fairly common practice for a Heinkel He 111Z *Zwilling* tug to assist the 323 into the air as all 11 engines strained at full throttle!

Such were the demands being made on the Luftwaffe's fast dwindling transport force in the final months of the War, it seems likely that the lumbering Messerschmitts continued working right up to the moment of extinction of the species.

Strategic Bomber – Heinkel He 177 Greif

The discontinuation of plans for a German strategic bombing force after General Walther Wever's death in 1936 has been referred to a number of times, yet a feeling that Germany might need a long range heavy bomber would never quite go away until the Reich faced overwhelming defeat in 1944. As early as 1938 the RLM tentatively approached Ernst Heinkel (the one 'bomber-maker' who had not produced a design for Wever's strategic bomber requirement) with an enquiry about a possible bomber capable of delivering 4,400 lb of bombs over a 1,000-mile radius–roughly twice the radius of the then-current He 111E. Preliminary drawings of the He 177 were complete before the end of that year, for a well-proportioned aircraft with four 1,000-hp Daimler-Benz DB 601s coupled in pairs, each pair in a single nacelle driving a single four-blade propeller. The prototype's first flight on November 19, 1939 lasted only 12 minutes as the pilot reported engine overheating, a trouble that was to plague the aircraft throughout its life. A remedy was tried by which additional radiators were fitted, but these added considerably to the aircraft's drag so that, to meet the range demands, extra fuel had to be carried–necessitating strengthening of the structure, adding weight, reducing performance, and so on. Accidents dogged the He 177 during its development phase, the second aircraft breaking up due to tail flutter during initial diving trials, the fourth aircraft failing to recover from a dive over a range in the Baltic and the fifth prototype being destroyed when its engines caught fire.

Despite universal dislike of the aircraft among all the Service pilots who flew development examples in 1940 and 1941, production got underway and some of the first operational He 177A-1 *Greif* (Griffon) bombers were delivered to *KG 40* at Bordeaux-Mérignac in July 1942, but further engine fires–usually on the ground following prolonged taxying at Bordeaux–resulted in the bestowal of the sobriquet *Luftwaffenfeuerzeug* ('the air force's fire-raiser'). The aircraft did however participate in a number of raids over Britain during the latter half of the year.

Numerous production variants followed, of which the A-3/R3 and R4, and A-5 could carry three Henschel Hs 293 anti-shipping weapons. These aircraft were flown by *III./KG 40*, commanded by Knight's Cross holder Major Rudolf Mons, at the end of 1943 when the Luftwaffe made determined attacks on Allied convoys plying between Britain and North Africa. In a memorable series of attacks on the 'double' convoy SL 139, northbound from Africa, *II./KG 40* launched a total of 28 Henschel Hs 293s, sinking one ship and damaging another, but losing no fewer than seven aircraft in combat and four aircraft in forced landings following engine fires; among the casualties was Major Mons himself. Thereafter the convoy attacks were switched to the hours of darkness when rather better results attended the attacks; one section of aircraft would drop flares along one side of the convoy while the main attacking force of He 177s launched its Hs 293s out of the darkness on the other side.

Meanwhile He 177s were being assembled to participate in Operation *Steinbock*, the so-called 'Little Blitz' launched against Britain early in 1944 under the command of Generalmajor Dietrich Peltz. Although this essentially symbolic venture is generally regarded as having been a wasteful failure, the Heinkel He 177s were flown to some effect. The tactics employed by the He 177A-5s of *I./KG 100*, commanded by Hauptmann von Kalkreuth, involved climbing to their maximum ceiling while still over German territory and setting course in a shallow dive so as to arrive over their target flying fast and low down; after releasing their bombs they made good their escape at maximum speed. These tactics certainly confused the defences and none

Following pages: *the He 177 bomber suffered many problems in service, not least those of engine fires; here a fire crew rush to tackle such a blaze, probably caused by overheating during prolonged ground running*

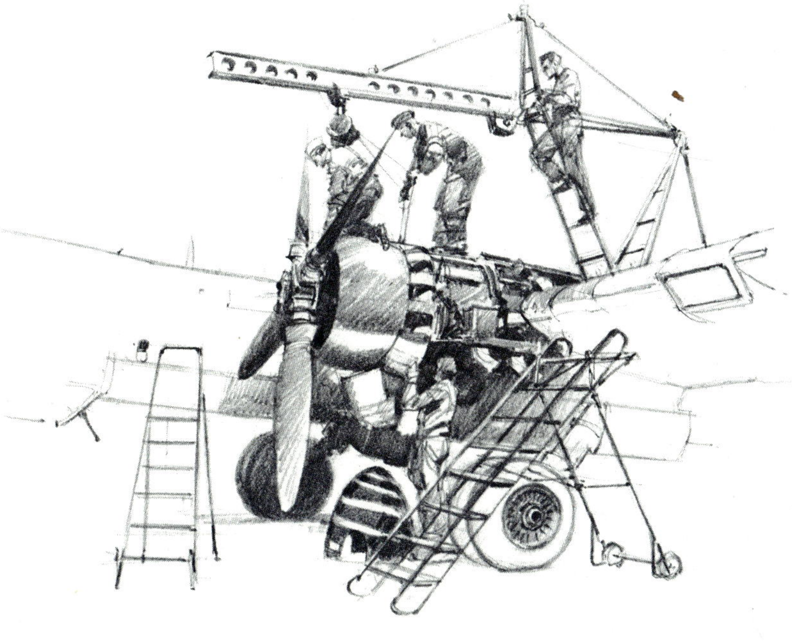

MICHAEL TURNER
'85

of *KG 100's* aircraft fell to Mosquito night fighters.

Some of the He 177's most spectacular but forlorn operations were flown by *Kampfgeschwader 1* <*Hindenburg*>, led by Oberstleutnant Horst von Riesen on the Russian Front during the late spring of 1944. With about 90 aircraft assembled on bases in East Prussia, von Riesen's force probably represented one of the most powerful that the Luftwaffe had managed to muster since the early months of Barbarossa. After a number of highly effective raids on genuinely strategic targets in Western Russia, Göring personally intervened to order the bombers against Soviet tanks–operations which exposed the big aircraft to the swarms of Russian fighters, achieved little in the way of tank destruction and resulted in the loss of more than 20 bombers.

Nevertheless when *KG 1* was eventually grounded, it had been defeated not by air combat but by Germany's mortal lack of fuel: to launch an attack by the Geschwader's 80 aircraft consumed 480 tons of fuel–equivalent to a single day's output from Germany's entire oil industry in the late summer of 1944.

The fundamental fault in the He 177 lay in Germany's lack of a powerful engine in 1938, capable of meeting the performance demands without the need to couple engines of lesser power. When more powerful engines became available the conventional 'four-nacelle' He 277 was produced–but 1944 was not the right time to start trying to build a strategic bomber force!

Reprisals against Britain – Dornier Do 217

The Dornier Do 217 was one of those unspectacular aeroplanes that, on account of almost trouble-free development, ready adaptability to perform many duties and rather better-than-average resistance to combat damage, remained in service with front line units from 1940 until the last weeks of the War.

A direct development of the Do 17, the Do 217 was

A Dornier Do 217 releases a Fritz X controlled-trajectory bomb; this weapon achieved spectacular results but required the aircraft to overfly its target thereby exposing it to gun defences

the outcome of a 1937 requirement issued by the RLM for a more versatile aircraft (classified as a heavy bomber) capable of reconnaissance and bombing over a much greater radius of action that its forerunner. With a pair of 1,075-hp DB 601 engines, the prototype was flown in August 1938 and pre-production aircraft were delivered in 1940 to the special long-range reconnaissance group, commanded by Oberstleutant Theodor Rowehl, for clandestine photographic and mapping missions over Russian territory throughout the winter months of 1940-41 as part of Hitler's preparations for the great attack on the Soviet Union.

The first major production variant was the Do 217E, of which most of the early examples were delivered to the relatively small number of bomber and anti-shipping Gruppen remaining in the West after the end of the Winter Blitz of 1940-41.

It was the Do 217Es of *KG 2* which flew most of the remaining small scale night raids over Britain during the late summer and autumn of 1941 and on which the RAF's slowly improving night fighter defences cut their teeth. Gone now were the relatively slow Do 17s and He 111s of the previous winter; instead the 330-mph Beaufighter had now to find and chase the 320-mph Do 217s, a task that all too frequently resulted in long stern chases over the sea, only to end when the German bomber put its nose down for base and escaped. By the end of the year all four Gruppen of *KG 2*, based at Eindhoven and Gilze-Rijen in Holland under Oberstleutnant Paul Weithus, were equipped with the bomber and, following the RAF's fire raid on the ancient Baltic port of Lübeck of 28/29 March 1942, Hitler ordered a series of *Terrorangriffe* (terror attacks) in reprisal against historic British cities and towns, in which *KG 2* was to take a major part. Forever known as the Baedeker raids (so called after the famous German travel guide books), the Luftwaffe's attacks constituted retaliation upon Bath, Birmingham, Cowes, Exeter, Grimsby, Hull, Middlesbrough, Norwich, Poole, Southampton, Weston-super-Mare and York, most of which were repeatedly attacked. Losses mounted steadily and by the end of September *KG 2* had only 23 left of the original 88 crews with which it opened the attacks. In four raids on towns in the English Midlands during the last week of July, for instance, the British defences brought down 27 aircraft–equivalent almost to an entire Gruppe.

During that summer Do 217s were also serving as night fighters over Germany, 217J-2s being used by seven Gruppen of *NJG 1, 3* and *4*, and J-1 intruders by *II.* and *III./NJG 2*. These were the forerunners of numerous other 217 night fighter variants which continued in service until the end of 1943, seldom returning the spectacular scores achieved by the Bf 110Gs and Ju 88 night fighters but nevertheless making a worthwhile contribution to the constant erosion of the RAF's bomber strength.

More spectacular however were the later anti-shipping operations by the Do 217Es, Ks and Ms, particularly those flown by *KG 100*. This Geschwader's *II.Gruppe*, based at Cognac, specialised with the Hs 293 rocket weapon, while the *III.Gruppe* at Marseilles carried the *Fritz X* controlled-trajectory armour-piercing bomb. Although *II.Gruppe* gained some minor successes at the end of August 1943, it was the Do 217K-2s of *III.Gruppe* which scored most effectively. On September 9 six aircraft attacked units of the Italian fleet as it sailed to join the Allies after the surrender by the Italian government. Hits were scored on the battleships *Roma* and *Italia*, the former being sunk with the loss of more than 1,200 lives. One week later the *Gruppenkommandeur*, Major Bernhard Jope (of Focke-Wulf Condor fame), obtained a direct hit on the battleship HMS *Warspite* off Salerno with a bomb that penetrated six decks before exploding, demolishing one boiler room and flooding four of the other five; it was for putting HMS *Warspite* out of action for almost a year that Jope was awarded his Oakleaves.

Later, after the Allies landed in Normandy, the Hs 293-carrying Do 217s of *KG 100* were turned against shore targets in Northern Europe. Some successes were chalked up, particularly against key river bridges, but losses to Allied night fighters mounted quickly and both *KG 2* and *KG 100* were disbanded in September 1944. The Dorniers launched their last weapons on April 12, 1945 in almost fruitless attacks on the bridges over the Oder river.

The Swallow and the Stormbird – Messerschmitt Me 262

Not only was Germany the first nation in the world to fly a turbojet-powered aircraft but she also retained that lead throughout the War. The experimental single-jet Heinkel He 178 was first flown by Flugkapitän Erich Warsitz at Marienehe airfield on August 27, 1939, but official interest in the aircraft was slow to materialise. Messerschmitt meanwhile had also been preparing preliminary schemes for jet aircraft, and by 1940 Junkers was working on an axial-flow turbojet, the 004, it being decided to produce a twin-jet fighter from the start. It was however to be Heinkel who first flew a jet aircraft designed from the outset as a fighter when the He 280 with a pair of Heinkel turbojets (producing only about 500 kg thrust each) was flown on April 2, 1941; this aircraft never attained production status.

Throughout the pre-flight development phase of the Messerschmitt Me 262 it was afforded relatively little priority. Even when it made its first jet-powered flight on July 18, 1942–having flown exactly one year previously with a piston engine in the nose–Germany was still riding the crest of the wave, with the massive surge forward into Russia. Barbarossa was not yet one month old. Even on the eve of Stalingrad only 60 aircraft had been ordered–all intended as fighters.

It was in November 1943 that Hitler watched a demonstration of the Me 262 and forthwith decreed that this aircraft would be just the weapon with which to carry out attacks on Britain, and ordered development to go ahead as a bomber. Although this order certainly diluted efforts to get the jet into service, Messerschmitt quietly went ahead with the fighter in parallel with the bomber and, following the increasingly heavy American daylight raids, Hitler finally agreed that the fighter should go ahead. This ill-informed interference by the Nazi leader probably delayed the entry of the Me 262 into service by at least nine months.

The performance of the Me 262 was certainly impressive–about 530 mph at 22,000 ft–and its heavy armament of four 30-mm cannon clearly reflected the pleas for more and bigger guns in fighters by Adolf Galland, at that time the Luftwaffe's Inspector General of Fighters. In mid-1944 Me 262 *Schwalbe* (Swallow) fighters joined the first semi-operational unit for evaluation, *Erprobungskommando 262 (EK 262)*, and in September, its work complete, this unit was disbanded and a fully operational unit, *Kommando Nowotny*, was formed with about 20 aircraft at Achmer and Hesepe. Early combats were disappointing as it soon emerged that the enormous difference in speed between the jet fighter and a lumbering B-17 or B-24 (a differential of well over 250 mph) made aiming and firing the *Schwalbe's* guns accurately extremely difficult, and the German pilots were accordingly slowing right down to attack the bombers –immediately sacrificing their great tactical advantage and putting themselves at the mercy of the P-47s and P-51s.

On November 8 Major Walter Nowotny was killed and his unit disbanded to provide the nucleus of a *Jagdgeschwader, JG 7 <Nowotny>*. Meanwhile Germany was being assailed not only by Allied heavy bombers but now by the entire arsenal of medium and even light bombers, and it was at the instigation of Galland that another unit came into existence, *Jagdverband 44*, with himself in command. Comprising such legendary pilots as Gerhard Barkhorn (who ultimately scored 301 victories during the War), Heinz Bär (220), Johannes Steinhoff (176), Walter Krupinski (197), Günther Lützow (108), Adolf Galland (104), Heinz Sachsenberg (104), Wolfgang Spätz (99), Siegfried Schnell (93), Hans Grünberg (82), Wilhelm Herget (72), Alfred Heckmann (71), Herbert

Following pages: *the jet that arrived just too late. An Me 262A-2a* Sturmvogel *from* KG 51 *streaks low over American ground forces during the campaign in the Ardennes*

MICHAEL TURNER
'85

Kaiser (68) and Hans-Ekkehard Bob (59)–each of whose victory scores far exceeded that of any Allied fighter pilot–*JV 44* was unquestionably the most talented assembly of fighter pilots ever seen. Unfortunately, although there was never any shortage of jet fighters, the problem lay in finding suitable bases that were not frequently bombed and strafed by Allied aircraft and, like the remainder of the Luftwaffe, *JV 44* was ultimately defeated by the lack of fuel.

Meanwhile the Me 262 bomber, the *Sturmvogel* ('Storm Bird') had entered service but, contrary to Hitler's former intentions, was never to attack Britain: the Allies had overrun all the Luftwaffe's bases within range of the British Isles. (Of all the German jets only the high altitude Arado Ar 234 reconnaissance aircraft ever flew over Britain.) Only relatively limited operations were flown by the *Sturmvogel*, for instance during the 'Battle of the Bulge' and against the Remagen Bridge, when the fast jets were able to attack and escape by reason of their high speed. However, following evaluation as a night fighter by Hajo Herrmann, now commanding *Jagddivision 30* (with *Wilde Sau* Wings), a number of Me 262 jets with *Lichtenstein SN-2* airborne radar served with *Kommando Welter* in the night defence of Berlin in the last weeks of the War.

Although the Germans had many problems with the Me 262 this remarkable aircraft was far in advance of anything the Allies had produced and, had its development not been hamstrung by Hitler's interference, the *Schwalbe* would certainly have taken a crippling toll of American bombers from late 1943 onwards.

Five Lancasters on the First Night – Heinkel He 219 UHU

That the Heinkel He 219 night fighter ever entered service during the War is remarkable in itself; that it should have rivalled the superb Mosquito is not so surprising for it was faster at all altitudes and, in most versions, carried a more powerful armament. Only in its less efficient radar was it in any way handicapped.

When first schemed as a private venture in mid-1940, the He 219 *Uhu* (Owl) was intended as a general

A Heinkel He 219A-5 brings its devastating battery of cannon to bear on an RAF Lancaster as the German night fighter crew penetrates a bomber stream in the final winter of the War

purpose fighter—in effect a cross between a *Zerstörer* and a pure interceptor. It was only when RAF Bomber Command's night raids began to reach substantial proportions in 1941 that the RLM sat up and took interest in the project and insisted that the aircraft go ahead as a dedicated night fighter. However although a prototype was first flown on November 15, 1942 virtually all the production design drawings were destroyed in an RAF Bomber Command raid on Rostock in the early spring of 1943.

In a monumental feat of administration entirely new sets of drawings were prepared and a production line established within six weeks at Vienna-Schwechat. Meanwhile several prototypes had flown and, in one of these, Werner Streib (who it will be remembered had been officially credited with the Luftwaffe's first night victory during 1940 in a Bf 110) was pitted in tests against a Junkers Ju 188S—a high-performance bomber with a top speed of 426 mph. The 219 demonstrated total superiority and Heinkel was awarded a contract for 300 aircraft by the RLM.

In April 1943 a small batch of pre-production He 219A-0s with *Lichtenstein SN-2* radar was given to *I./NJG 1* at Venlo in Holland for preliminary operational trials armed with a variety of different gun combinations. On the very first combat sortie, flown by Streib once again, on the night of June 11/12, the 219 penetrated a bomber stream heading for Münster and in the space of 30 minutes had destroyed five Lancasters with his armament of six 20-mm cannon. On landing however Streib found that his hydraulics had been shot away and in a flapless landing his aircraft broke up—fortunately without injury to the crew. Perhaps more significant were the six Mosquitos shot down by Streib's pilots in the next ten days—a hitherto unheard-of feat in the air war over Germany.

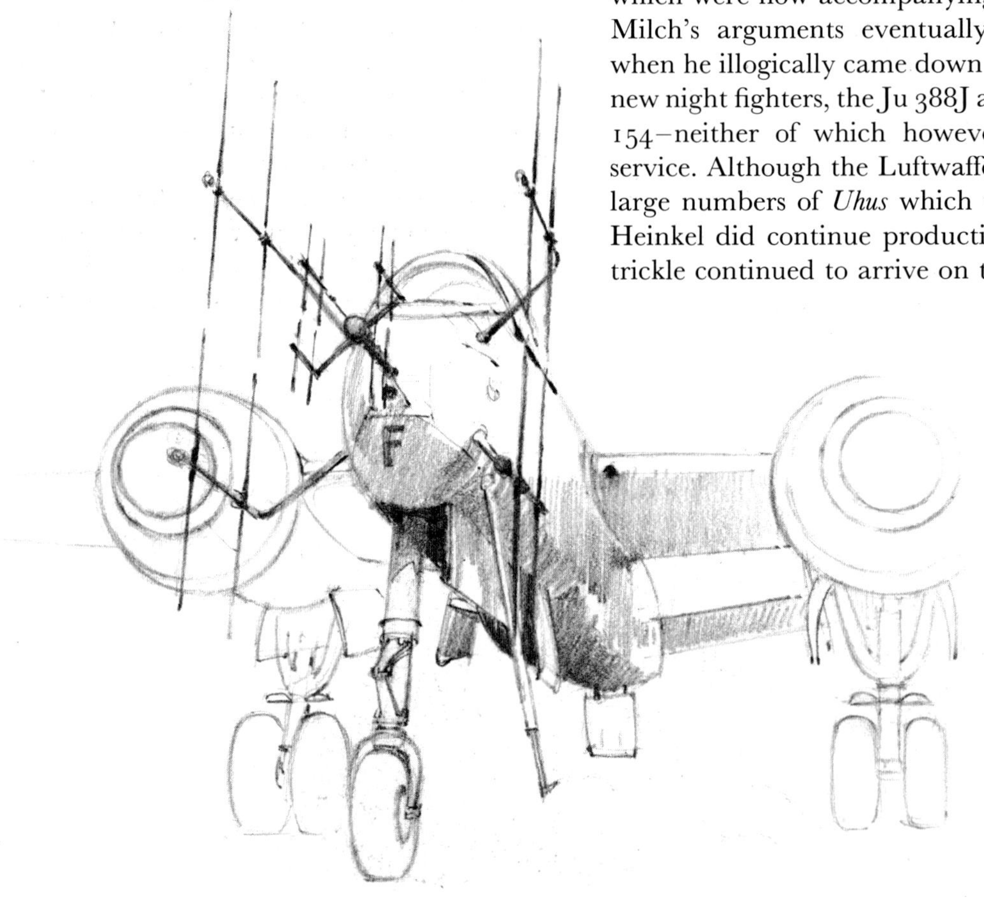

The first major production version was the 219A-5 which usually carried an armament of two 30-mm and two 20-mm guns, but this was superseded in 1944 by the A-7 which carried an armament of no fewer than eight cannon, comprising two 30-mm guns in the wing roots, four 20-mm guns in a ventral tray and two upward-firing 30-mm guns in a *Schräge Musik* installation. It was as this deadly fighter was entering service with *NJG 1* that Feldmarschall Erhard Milch, Chief of Aircraft Production, recommended discontinuation of He 219 production on the grounds that it diluted production effort on the Junkers Ju 88G night fighter which was shown to be well able to counter such RAF bombers as the Halifax and Lancaster, and was established in widespread production. He overlooked the fact that the Ju 88 was itself highly vulnerable to the Mosquito, increasing numbers of which were now accompanying the bomber streams. Milch's arguments eventually prevailed, but only when he illogically came down in favour of two other new night fighters, the Ju 388J and the Focke-Wulf Ta 154—neither of which however were to see much service. Although the Luftwaffe was thus deprived of large numbers of *Uhus* which were eagerly awaited, Heinkel did continue production unofficially, and a trickle continued to arrive on the night fighter units.

The only other unit to receive a significant number of He 219s was the special 'anti-Mosquito' *Gruppe*, *Nachtjagdgruppe 10*, based at Werneuchen under Major Rudolf Schönert to protect Berlin. Schönert, who ended the War with the Oakleaves and 64 night victories, served operational tours on *NJG 1, 2, 3, 5, 10* and *100* between 1941 and 1945, and flew almost every type of night fighter to enter service with the Luftwaffe. His He 219s comprised a mixture of A-7s and B-2s with power boosting which gave the aircraft a top speed of over 430 mph for short periods.

Taking all known claims and losses into account it seems likely that *Uhus* accounted for a total of rather more than 100 Mosquitos between September 1944 and the end of the War. Unfortunately, such was the devastating effect of the 219's gun armament that many of its victims blew up with such shattering effect that quite a large number of the German night fighter crews were lost in the explosion or when their aircraft was hit by debris. Nevertheless one can only speculate how much greater the RAF's loss would have been had it not been for Milch's ill-advised interference. As it was, only 268 of these superlative fighters were ever built.

The Last Blitz – Arado Ar 234 Blitz

Less widely exposed to the attention of Western observers at the end of the War than the Me 262, was the Arado Ar 234. This originated in 1941 and started a train of tactical philosophy that was to engender the RAF post-War Canberra–an aeroplane that still performed a useful function in the 1980s!

Encouraged by early work on German turbojet engines the Arado design team forwarded to the RLM a scheme for a twin-jet shoulder-wing aircraft powered by two Junkers 004B engines, capable of carrying a pair of 550-lb bombs and at a speed of over 400 mph–a speed that rendered defensive gun armament superfluous. Production of the engines was however slow and it was not until June 15, 1943 that the first prototype made its maiden flight, with Flugkapitän Selle at the controls. As originally designed the Ar 234 dispensed with conventional landing gear, being flown off a jettisonable three-wheel trolley for take-off and landing on three retractable skids. This system was thought likely to give rise to problems when the aircraft reached the operational squadrons and was abandoned, the production Ar 234B being provided with a tricycle undercarriage–by 1943 generally recognised as virtually essential for all jet-powered aircraft. Conventional as this feature was the Ar 234 *Blitz* (Lightning) introduced for the first time in a high performance operational aircraft an ejector seat for the pilot, in effect a mechanical catapult intended to enable him to clear the tail if forced to abandon the aircraft when flying at high speed. The Ar 234Bs, of which the first were completed in the summer of 1944, comprised B-1 reconnaissance aircraft and the B-2 bomber, the latter with a three-axis autopilot, bombing computer, tachometric bombsight, pressure cabin, ejector seat and landing drag parachutes–extremely advanced features that were as yet scarcely being considered, let alone used in Allied aircraft during the War. The aircraft often employed Walter rockets to assist take-off, particularly when loaded to the maximum with two 2,200-lb bombs.

Most of the early operations in the second half of 1944 however involved reconnaissance work, including many flights by the *Versuchsverband Oberbefehlshaber der Luftwaffe* (Air Force C-in-C's Special Unit) over the United Kingdom. These sorties were flown at around 30,000 ft and high speed, giving complete immunity from interception efforts by the RAF and USAAF, a fact that the Allied authorities were distinctly shy of admitting!

Early in 1945 *1./Versuchsverb.Ob.d.L* and two other Ar 234B-1 reconnaissance units were disbanded to provide the nucleus of pilots for three regular line units, *1.(F)/100* and *1.(F)/123* at Rheine, and *1.(F)/33* at Aalborg in Denmark, and Stavanger in Norway, the latter continuing the flights over Britain right up to the end of the War.

One other Ar 234B-1 unit was formed in Northern Italy following complaints by the Wehrmacht that it was being starved of reconnaissance and that Allied forces had total freedom of movement without the slightest effort being made to report it by the Luftwaffe. This unit was *Kommando Sommer*, named

Loaded with a pair of 1,100-lb bombs under the engine nacelles an Arado Ar 234B-2 of KG 76 *blasts off an autobahn during the Battle of the Bulge, assisted by Walter rockets*

after its commanding officer, Hauptmann Joachim Sommer, one of the very small number of Luftwaffe reconnaissance pilots to be awarded the Knight's Cross (in December 1944). He had at his disposal just four Ar 234B-1s with which to cover the whole of Italy, a task he accomplished with great skill, flying numerous photographic missions at around 40,000 ft–once more without interference. Despite the fact that all the engines in the Arados had to undergo major maintenance or removal after only 10 hours' flying, Sommer contrived to keep at least one aircraft permanently available, day and night.

Meanwhile the Ar 234B-2 bomber had entered service with *KG 76* under Oberstleutnant Robert Kowalewski, who had won the Knight's Cross at the beginning of the 1940-41 Blitz against Britain. Despite the growing fuel crisis that threatened to paralyse German air operations over the Western Front from December 1944 onwards, *KG 76's* jets entered combat during the Battle of the Bulge and later joined Me 262 *Stürmvogel* bombers in the desperate attempts to destroy the key Ludendorg bridge at Remagen in March 1945. RAF pilots recall that the fast, low-flying Arados were virtually impossible to shoot down from the air, unless one was fortunate to catch one in the landing circuit at its base. Similar luck was needed to destroy them with light ack-ack guns; the half-dozen that fell to the guns on the grould all fell to 40-mm Bofors using proximity-fused shells that had been introduced to combat the flying bombs.

Arado had done a great deal of development work on the 234, and produced several versions with four jet engines, but these were still far from service status when Germany surrendered.

Only a Flea, but Oh-Oh – Messerschmitt Me 163 Komet

The tiny Komet rocket interceptor's arrival in limited service with the Luftwaffe in 1944 was the climax of a research and development programme that is still unique in history, for no other nation has ever succeeded in persuading its air force that a manned aeroplane powered solely by a rocket motor represented a realistic means of intercepting bombers. To do so the technicians and pilots associated with the Me 163 had to contend with tremendous personal risk owing to the critical instability of the fuels involved, mishandling of which–however fractionally the limits of usage were overstepped–all too often resulted in shattering explosion and truly astonishing devastation. With its combat speed of close to 600 mph and pair of heavy guns the Me 163 eventually equipped a special *Jagdgeschwader* whose official badge was inscribed '*Wie ein Floh, aber Oho!*' (Only a flea, but oh-oh!)

Research into rocket propulsion for aircraft originated in work carried out in great secrecy in Germany during the 1920s at much the same time that Dr Alexander Lipisch was experimenting with tailless aircraft. In due course the promising results of these two fields of research encouraged a number of

manufacturers to start investigating the possibility of evolving high-performance rocket-powered military aircraft, among which were the DFS 39 and 40, and the Heinkel He 176. A Messerschmitt prototype, the Me 163, was completed during the winter of 1940-41, although no suitable rocket was yet available. Starting in the spring of 1941 this little aircraft, with modestly swept-back wing with fixed slots and a single vertical tail surface, underwent handling trials as a glider before being delivered to the experimental establishment at Peenemünde on the Baltic coast for the installation of a Walter rocket motor. This motor worked on the cold principle, employing the interaction of the propellants *T-Stoff* (80 per cent hydrogen peroxide and 20 per cent water) and *C-Stoff* (methyl alcohol, hydrazine hydrate and water). During development of these fuels there were several massive explosions, on one occasion demolishing an entire block of laboratories at Peenemünde.

When powered flights by Heini Dittmar started in the autumn the maximum quantity of fuel carried (2,640 lb) was consumed in just over two minutes at full throttle, so the Me 163 was towed up to about 12,000 ft by a Bf 110 before casting off and starting the motor; however after reaching a speed of over 620 mph Dittmar had to cut the rocket as the compressibility shock threatened to send the aircraft into an uncontrolled dive.

Soon after these flights–on which the official world air speed record was far exceeded–the RLM ordered military prototypes which came to be tested by some of the most eminent fighter pilots, including Oberst Gordon Gollob (who was a member of the Fighter Staff of the OKL and also test flew the Me 262 and He 162), Major Wolfgang Späte and Major Robert Olejnik. By early 1943 pre-production Me 163B-0s were being equipped with their armament of two 30-mm cannon for operational evaluation by Service pilots at Peenemünde. Led by Späte–until an inexplicable posting to command a fighter squadron on the Russian Front–this unit comprised pilots of enormous experience, including Oberleutnant Josef Pöhs (killed on December 30, 1943), Olejnik, Hauptmann Toni Thaler, Feldwebel Alois Wörndl (killed early in 1944) and others.

Gradually this hardcore of pilots evolved tactics for operations against large bomber formations, being essentially simple in theory but fraught with hazard in

Its rocket fuel exhausted and its attack complete, a Me 163 dives out of gun range from a B-17 Fortress formation during the great American daylight bombing offensive of 1944

practice. With less than 4 minutes' fuel available, the Me 163 had to be positioned on its runway, awaiting the approach of a bomber formation, until either the bombers or their condensation trails were visible to the waiting pilot. After performing the tricky start-up he would roar off down the runway, jettisoning his two-wheel trolley after lift-off, and pull up into a full-throttle near-vertical climb, but then throttling back to avoid exceeding about 500 mph. Hopefully he would arrive in a position to make a single firing pass at a bomber (or even two, if the formation of bombers was no higher than 20,000 ft). His motor would cut out and, provided he was not already being boxed-in by escorting fighters, he would dive away–hopefully being able to spot his base where he'd carry out a dead-stick landing on the under-fuselage skid. In conditions of poor visibility some pilots had to bale out–no easy accomplishment in a fast-gliding Me 163!

In May 1944 *Jagdgeschwader 400* started forming at Wittmundhaven under Olejnik, and the following month its first three Staffeln *(I./JG 400)* moved to Brandis, near Leipzig. They had their first taste of action on August 16 against B-17s but failed to score. *II.* and *III.Gruppen* were formed before the end of the year but neither was fully operational when the War ended. Although about 300 Komets were produced, their total number of confirmed victories reached only 14, of which 10 were B-17s, two B-24s, a B-26 and a Mosquito (the latter shot down by 'Bubi' Glogner); one of the B-17s was shot down by Leutnant Fritz Kelb of a trials unit, using unique vertically-fired 50-mm shells.

So ended a remarkable chapter of endeavour which was probably doomed more by the hopeless situation in which Germany found herself in the last year of the War than by any lack of skill, determination or bravery.

The People's Fighter – Heinkel HE 162 Salamander

When it became clear to the RLM in mid-1944 that plans to put the Me 262 and Me 163 fighters into mass production quickly would be unlikely to be fulfilled–and the RLM itself was subjected to sweeping reorganisation to give staunch Nazi party officials positions of greater influence–the possibility of introducing a low-cost, mass-production fighter was

raised. Originator of this idea was Dipl.-Ing Karl-Otto Saur, whose post now carried the title of Chief Official Administrator and Head of the Office of the German Ministry of War Equipment and Munitions, a man of influence but almost lacking in aeronautical qualification. With the catch-phrase title *Volksjäger* ('People's Fighter') this proposal was put to the aircraft industry on September 8, 1944 together with stipulations that the aircraft must employ a minimum of stategic materials, must weigh not more than 2,000 kg, possess an endurance of not less than 30 minutes and a performance greater than any Allied fighter, while using the 1,760-lb thrust BMW 109-003 jet engine.

Several design proposals were put forward, and despite the Blohm und Voss tender being generally regarded as the best, Heinkel was awarded the production contract on September 23, the same day that Göring announced that supplies of pilots for the new fighter would be drawn from the Hitler Youth–most of their flying training being completed on the *single-seat* jets!

The Germans were unable to bring the little He 162 interceptor into service; two such aircraft of I./JG 1 *are shown here in a hangar at Leck in the last days of the War*

As plans to produce 4,000 He 162 each month by mid-1945 were drawn up by Generalkommisar Philipp Kessler (the organising genius who had totally re-established Germany's ball-bearing industry in three months after the Schweinfurt bombings), construction of the prototype fighter began on September 24. Despite the popular name *Volksjäger*–only generally found in government records–the aircraft was known as the *Spatz* (sparrow) by the aircraft industry, and as the *Salamander* (the animal reputedly able to live in fire) by the Luftwaffe. Of radical appearance the little aeroplane was built almost entirely of wood with shoulder wing, nosewheel landing gear and twin fins and rudders. The single turbojet was mounted on top of the fuselage behind the cockpit.

The prototype was first flown by Flugkapitän Peter at Vienna-Schwechat on December 6, a flight marred only by the loss of a wheel door owing to defective wood bonding; the remedies had not been applied when, on December 10 in front of numerous officials, Peter was killed when one wing of the He 162 disintegrated–again following bonding failure. Other modifications were also now put in hand including enlarging the tail surfaces and angling-down the wing tips. By the end of January all 10 of the initial development aircraft from Vienna-Schwechat had flown (a feat unparalleled anywhere and rendered all the more astonishing having regard to the chaotic conditions prevailing in Germany). These and further development aircraft underwent hurried evalution by Rechlin pilots who reported favourably, nevertheless pointing to the fact that even experienced pilots had to handle the *Salamander* smoothly (tacitly ridiculing Göring's vision of thousands of schoolboys confronting RAF and USAAF Tempests, Mosquitos, P-51s and other adversaries).

Already the first Luftwaffe He 162 unit, *Erprobungskommando 162*, led by Oberstleutnant Heinz Bär (220 victories and holder of the Swords), had been formed in January 1944 to train pilots and groundcrews at Rechlin–the pilots indeed being men of considerable combat experience. In February the first fighter *Geschwader*, *JG* < *Oesau* >, started converting to He 162s under Oberst Herbert Ihlefeldt (130 victories, and also a holder of the Swords); two of its Gruppen eventually received about 50 aircraft and by the end of April was on the verge of becoming combat-ready when it had to move from its base at Warnemünde owing to the approach of the Red Army.

Detailed examination of Allied records suggest that there were about 30 sightings of the *Salamander* by RAF and USAAF fighter pilots but it seems that on almost every occasion the German pilot was on a training flight, and was under orders not to engage but to make use of his speed and escape. With a top speed of about 520 mph it was at least comparable to that of the Me 262. In the two separate instances in which a Tempest and a P-51 engaged He 162s neither of the Allied pilots could open fire before the He 162 made off.

Desperately trying to find fuel, the last elements of *JG 1* assembled at Leck finally surrendering on May 8. When eventually the Allies searched the many improvised underground aircraft factories throughout Germany, among the vast quantity of war matériel found were almost 800 He 162s in the final stages of completion. One must assume that Göring's nightmare plan was only narrowly averted.

Twin-engined Dornier Do 335

In the Front Line of Democracy

The Post-war Luftwaffe and the Tornado

The final unconditional surrender of Germany in May 1945 came about as the result of total occupation by the Allies from the West and East, her armed forces overwhelmed or paralysed, her industries destroyed, her politics reviled, and her former leaders dead, cringing or in captivity awaiting trial.

Retribution followed as the Allies partitioned the nation into two, neither component permitted to manufacture machines of war. Yet within 10 years of the War's end distrust and covert hostility had set in between East and West, and both great power blocs were hard at work to create military infrastructures on the assumed principle of collective defence against the other. Germany lay between.

And with every European nation, emerging from economic and social devastation and paying lip service to this collective defence–yet contributing the moral minimum in actual military strength in the interests of domestic political stability–both elements of the divided Germany were encouraged to contribute to the military strength of their respective blocs.

West Germany's new Luftwaffe was once more born again, but in the mid-1950s it suffered two fundamental handicaps: a 10-year gap in the active participation in aviation research at a time when technology advanced at an unprecedented pace, and the loss of a generation of trained personnel. In a more liberal world–compared with the attitudes adopted following the First World War–the German people were free, indeed encouraged to rebuild their nation according to democratic precepts. However popular attitudes, opposed to any form of reborn militarism, were fairly widespread and an aircraft industry stood low among national priorities.

Thus between the mid-1950s and the mid-1960s the new air force was weaned on foreign aircraft, principally from America, as new factories were built and their engineers re-learned old skills and trained in the new. In due course the Luftwaffe assumed an autonomous identity within NATO and, to a large extent promoted by American vested interests and familiarity with American products, opted to adopt a modern aircraft, the Lockheed F-104*G* Starfighter, as its main combat aircraft, eventually building this very advanced aeroplane under licence.

Despite prolonged growing pains the Starfighter not only survived but served for 20 years both with the Luftwaffe and the Kriegsmarine.

Above: *Lockheed F-104G Starfighter*

It was in 1968 that several of the NATO partners, the Federal Republic of West Germany among them, formed a consortium to evolve a replacement for the Starfighter to enter service early in the 1980s. Such was the likely cost and complexity of this 'multi-rôle combat aircraft (MRCA) that most of the consortium backed out at various stages, leaving Germany and Italy to continue. However Britain–whose partnership in a similar project with France had collapsed–joined the MRCA consortium, and so the multi-national Panavia Tornado was born.

This enterprise, involving expenditure by the three nations of £30bn over twenty years, was to constitute the biggest international military project ever undertaken in Europe, ultimately resulting in the production of some 350 aircraft each for the air forces of Germany and the RAF, and one hundred for Italy. Roughly half the British aircraft would be interceptor fighters but all the remainder would be multi-rôle strike aircraft.

Germany's Tornados entered service in 1982, their crews being trained at a Tri-National Training Establishment in Britain but then going on to serve with four Geschwader of the Luftwaffe and two of the Kriegsmarine. That the Tornado represents one of the most advanced military aircraft in the world in its class is undisputed, being designed especially for the NATO war scenario to deliver its weapons at very low level, at high speed and with unprecedented accuracy, and possessing the ability to survive all manner of modern sophisticated warfare in an environment of extensive enemy electronic countermeasures.

It was with a fine sense of history that the first fully operational *Jagdbombergeschwader*, *JG 31*, to be re-formed with the Tornado in Luftwaffe service carried the honour title <*Boelcke*>. Though Germany's great air force may have twice suffered privation in the wilderness in the last 70 years, who can gainsay the strength of tradition and loyalty that has flourished throughout?

Left: *such was post-War recovery of the aircraft industry that Germany could probably have produced the superb Panavia Tornado strike aircraft by itself; only the enormous cost demanded tri-national collaboration*

Below: *Fiat G 91*

Explanation of Terms

A characteristic of the German language is its plethora of 'portmanteau' nouns – the coupling together of two or more components to create a single word of often awesome proportions to fully describe the root noun; this is particularly commonplace in the military vocabulary. The German Air Force features the *Geschwader* (or Wing) as its basic operational administrative formation. It is almost invariably qualified by its operational duty by the prefixing of such words as *Jagd* (fighter or, literally, 'hunt'), *Kampf* (bomber or, confusingly, 'battle'), *Aufklärungs* (reconnaissance or 'explaining'), *Lehr* (training), and so on. Sometimes a further qualification, such as *Nacht*, *Schnell* or *See* (respectively night, high speed or maritime) is added as well. Thus *Schnellkampfgeschwader* is a 'high-speed bomber wing'. This practice survives to this day, and the *Jagbombergeschwader* (in usage contracted to JBG or *Jabo*), the fighter-bomber wing, is the basis of the modern *Luftwaffe*.

A *Geschwader* in the Second World War comprised about 110 aircraft and for theatre deployment was divided into three or four (occasionally five) *Gruppen* (Groups), invariably denoted by prefixed Roman numerals, plus a *Geschwaderstab* flight (Wing Staff Flight), comprising the *Geschwaderkommodore* (Wing Commodore), his adjutant, technical, intelligence and other staff officers, all of whom were usually operational pilots.

Each *Gruppe* was an autonomous formation and constituted a self-sufficient entity for operational purposes, during the War often being deployed from theatre to theatre with or without the remainder of the Wing. Occasionally each *Gruppe* within the *Geschwader* would be tasked differently; for example the Operational Training Wing, *Lehrgeschwader 1*, comprised I., II. and III. *Gruppen* of Ju 88 bombers, *IV.(Stuka) Gruppe*, and *V.(Zerstörer) Gruppe*, the latter equipped with 'destroyer' fighters.

Finally, each *Gruppe* was divided into three *Staffeln* (approximately, squadrons and denoted by prefixed Arabic numerals) and a *Stabskette* (Staff section), each being flown tactically as *Ketten* or *Schwärme* (in practice two or three 'sections' of four aircraft).

Command ranks of these operational units varied widely, the German equivalent being generally one rank junior to that in the Allied air forces. The *Geschwaderkommodore* would usually be an *Oberst* (full colonel) on a bomber unit or an *Oberstleutnant* (lieutenant-colonel) on a fighter Wing; a Major (*Gruppenkommandeur*) would often command a *Gruppe*, and a *Hauptmann* (captain) a *Staffel* as the *Staffelkapitän*. When a *Staffelkäpitan* was absent for any reason his place would be taken by his deputy as the *Staffelführer* ('squadron leader') – who might be an *Oberleutnant* (first lieutenant).

One of the oddities of the Second World War, the Blohm und Voss Bv 144 army co-operation aircraft

Index